THE ROAD TO KITTY HAWK

TIME
LIFE ®
BOOKS

Other Publications:
THE GOOD COOK
THE SEAFARERS
THE ENCYCLOPEDIA OF COLLECTIBLES
THE GREAT CITIES
WORLD WAR II
HOME REPAIR AND IMPROVEMENT
THE WORLD'S WILD PLACES
THE TIME-LIFE LIBRARY OF BOATING
HUMAN BEHAVIOR
THE ART OF SEWING
THE OLD WEST
THE EMERGENCE OF MAN
THE AMERICAN WILDERNESS
THE TIME-LIFE ENCYCLOPEDIA OF GARDENING
LIFE LIBRARY OF PHOTOGRAPHY
THIS FABULOUS CENTURY
FOODS OF THE WORLD
TIME-LIFE LIBRARY OF AMERICA
TIME-LIFE LIBRARY OF ART
GREAT AGES OF MAN
LIFE SCIENCE LIBRARY
THE LIFE HISTORY OF THE UNITED STATES
TIME READING PROGRAM
LIFE NATURE LIBRARY
LIFE WORLD LIBRARY

FAMILY LIBRARY:
HOW THINGS WORK IN YOUR HOME
THE TIME-LIFE BOOK OF THE FAMILY CAR
THE TIME-LIFE FAMILY LEGAL GUIDE
THE TIME-LIFE BOOK OF FAMILY FINANCE

THE ROAD TO KITTY HAWK

by Valerie Moolman

AND THE EDITORS OF TIME-LIFE BOOKS

TIME-LIFE BOOKS, ALEXANDRIA, VIRGINIA

Time-Life Books Inc.
is a wholly owned subsidiary of

TIME INCORPORATED

FOUNDER: Henry R. Luce 1898-1967

Editor-in-Chief: Henry Anatole Grunwald
Chairman of the Board: Andrew Heiskell
President: James R. Shepley
Editorial Director: Ralph Graves
Vice Chairman: Arthur Temple

TIME-LIFE BOOKS INC.

MANAGING EDITOR: Jerry Korn
Executive Editor: David Maness
Assistant Managing Editors: Dale M. Brown (planning),
George Constable, George G. Daniels (acting), Martin Mann,
John Paul Porter
Art Director: Tom Suzuki
Chief of Research: David L. Harrison
Director of Photography: Robert G. Mason
Senior Text Editor: Diana Hirsh
Assistant Art Director: Arnold C. Holeywell
Assistant Chief of Research: Carolyn L. Sackett
Assistant Director of Photography: Dolores A. Littles

CHAIRMAN: Joan D. Manley
President: John D. McSweeney
Executive Vice Presidents: Carl G. Jaeger,
John Steven Maxwell, David J. Walsh
Vice Presidents: George Artandi (comptroller);
Stephen L. Bair (legal counsel); Peter G. Barnes;
Nicholas Benton (public relations); John L. Canova;
Beatrice T. Dobie (personnel); Carol Flaumenhaft
(consumer affairs); Nicholas J. C. Ingleton (Asia);
James L. Mercer (Europe/South Pacific); Herbert Sorkin
(production); Paul R. Stewart (marketing)

THE EPIC OF FLIGHT

Editorial Staff for *The Road to Kitty Hawk*
Editor: Thomas H. Flaherty Jr.
Designer: Albert Sherman
Chief Researcher: Pat Good
Picture Editor: Richard Kenin
Text Editor: Russell B. Adams Jr.
Staff Writers: Bobbie Conlan, Lee Hassig, John Manners,
C. Tyler Mathisen
Researchers: Patti H. Cass and Carol Forsyth Mickey
(principals), Susan Schneider Blair
Assistant Designer: Van W. Carney
Editorial Assistant: Kathy Wicks

Editorial Production
Production Editor: Douglas B. Graham
Operations Manager: Gennaro C. Esposito, Gordon E. Buck
(assistant)
Assistant Production Editor: Feliciano Madrid
Quality Control: Robert L. Young (director), James J. Cox
(assistant), Daniel J. McSweeney, Michael G. Wight
(associates)
Art Coordinator: Anne B. Landry
Copy Staff: Susan B. Galloway (chief), Elise Ritter Gibson,
Elizabeth Graham, Sheirazada Hann, Cynthia Kleinfeld,
Celia Beattie
Picture Department: Nan Cromwell Scott

Correspondents: Elisabeth Kraemer (Bonn); Margot
Hapgood, Dorothy Bacon, Lesley Coleman (London); Susan
Jonas, Lucy T. Voulgaris (New York); Maria Vincenza Aloisi,
Josephine du Brusle (Paris); Ann Natanson (Rome). Valuable
assistance was provided by Nakanori Tashiro, Asia Editor,
Tokyo. The editors also wish to thank Martha Mader (Bonn);
Karin Pearce (London); Carolyn T. Chubet, Miriam Hsia,
Christina Lieberman (New York); M. T. Hirschkoff (Paris);
Mimi Murphy (Rome).

THE AUTHOR
Valerie Moolman, a former text editor for
Time-Life Books, is the author of 40 books,
documentary film scripts and dramatic shows
on subjects that range from aviation to social history. *The Road to Kitty Hawk* is her
first Time-Life book.

THE CONSULTANT for *The Road to Kitty Hawk*
Tom D. Crouch is Curator of Aeronautics
at the National Air and Space Museum in
Washington, D.C. He holds a Ph.D. from
Ohio State University and is the author of
several books and numerous articles on the
history of aviation.

THE CONSULTANTS for *The Epic of Flight*
Melvin B. Zisfein, the principal consultant, is
Deputy Director of the National Air and
Space Museum, Washington. He received
degrees in aeronautical engineering from the
Massachusetts Institute of Technology and
has contributed to many scientific, techno-
logical and historical publications. He is an
Associate Fellow of the American Institute of
Aeronautics and Astronautics.

Charles Harvard Gibbs-Smith, Research Fellow at the Science Museum, London, and
a Keeper-Emeritus of the Victoria and Albert Museum, London, has written or edited
some 20 books and numerous articles on
aeronautical history. In 1978 he served as the
first Lindbergh Professor of Aerospace History at the National Air and Space Museum,
Smithsonian Institution, Washington.

Dr. Hidemasa Kimura, honorary professor at
Nippon University, Tokyo, is the author of
numerous books on the history of aviation
and is a widely known authority on aeronautical engineering and aircraft design. One
plane that he designed established a world
distance record in 1938.

For information about any Time-Life book, please write:
Reader Information
Time-Life Books
541 North Fairbanks Court
Chicago, Illinois 60611

Library of Congress Cataloguing in Publication Data
Moolman, Valerie.
    The road to Kitty Hawk.
    (The Epic of flight; 3)
    Bibliography: p.
    Includes index.
    1. Aeronautics—History. I. Time-Life Books.
II. Title. III. Series: Epic of flight; 3.
TL515.M63   629.13'009   79-21943
ISBN 0-8094-3260-9
ISBN 0-8094-3259-5 lib. bdg.

CONTENTS

Man's soaring dream

"O that I had wings like a dove, for then I would fly away and be at rest." Few urges have so inspired, and frustrated, mankind as the desire to fly. From the earliest of times, kings and commoners, the enlightened and the ignorant—and the Old Testament psalmist quoted above—have shared an envy of the ease with which birds cruise the skies. For centuries, the fantasy of soaring, of breaking earthly bonds and mastering the winds, has exerted so fundamental a drive that it seems somehow woven into the fabric of humanity. In art and literature, in mythology and religion, man has pondered and marveled at—even worshipped—the phenomenon of flight.

For a few men of ingenuity and science, however, flight was more than a subject for speculation and wonder: It commanded serious study. Generations of inventive men designed—and occasionally constructed—model flying machines; some of the more notable and unusual products of their imagination are shown on these and the following pages. Each of these contraptions, though studiously conceived, was ultimately doomed to confirm the adage of the skeptics—which survived into the dawn of the 20th Century—that Man Will Never Fly.

Fortunately, neither failure nor ridicule deterred the dreamers and the inventors. "The wits will tell me that I am flighty," wrote Thomas Walker, a 19th Century Englishman whose birdlike contrivance appears on pages 12-13, "but I do not write for such folks. Columbus was laughed at when he talked of a continent beyond the Atlantic; but flighty as he might appear, he found it and wise men lost it!" Thomas Walker sought in vain to fly. But with a gallant company of other earth-bound innovators, he left guiding footprints on the road that eventually led to Kitty Hawk.

The beaked and befeathered Passarola, or great bird, designed by Portuguese priest Laurenço de Gusmão, is detailed in this engraving made in 1709. Magnets encased in metal globes were supposed to help lift the great bird.

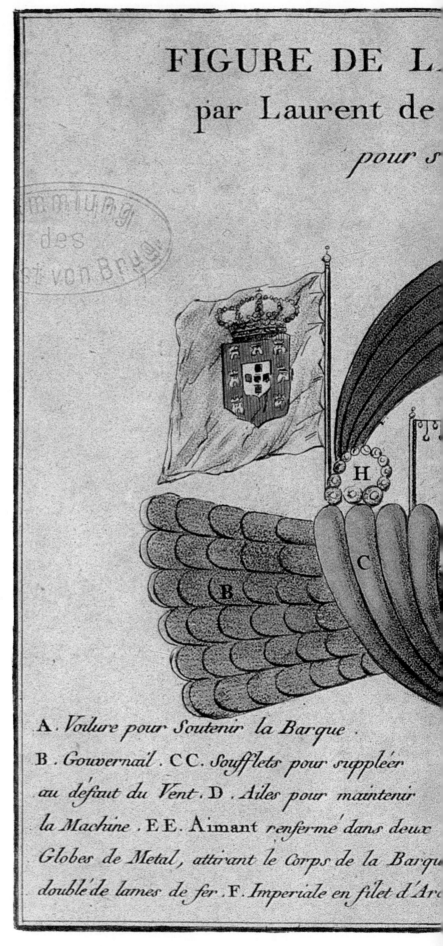

FIGURE DE L

par Laurent de

pour s

H

B

C

A. *Voilure pour Soutenir la Barque.*

B. *Gouvernail.* C C. *Soufflets pour suppléer au défaut du Vent.* D. *Ailes pour maintenir la Machine.* E E. *Aimant renfermé dans deux Globes de Metal, attirant le Corps de la Barque double de lames de fer.* F. *Imperiale en filet d'Ar*

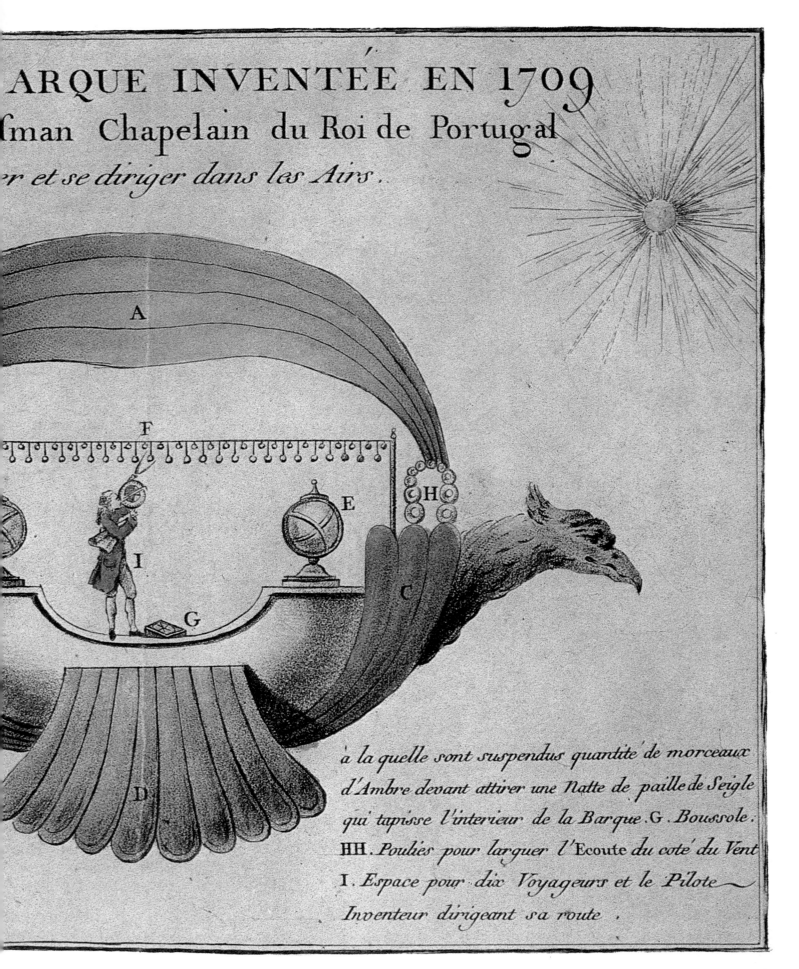

ARQUE INVENTÉE EN 1709

Iman Chapelain du Roi de Portugal

r et se diriger dans les Airs.

à la quelle sont suspendus quantité de morceaux
d'Ambre devant attirer une Natte de paille de Seigle
qui tapisse l'interieur de la Barque. G. Boussole.
HH. Poulies pour larguer l'Ecoute du coté du Vent
I. Espace pour dix Voyageurs et le Pilote
Inventeur dirigeant sa route.

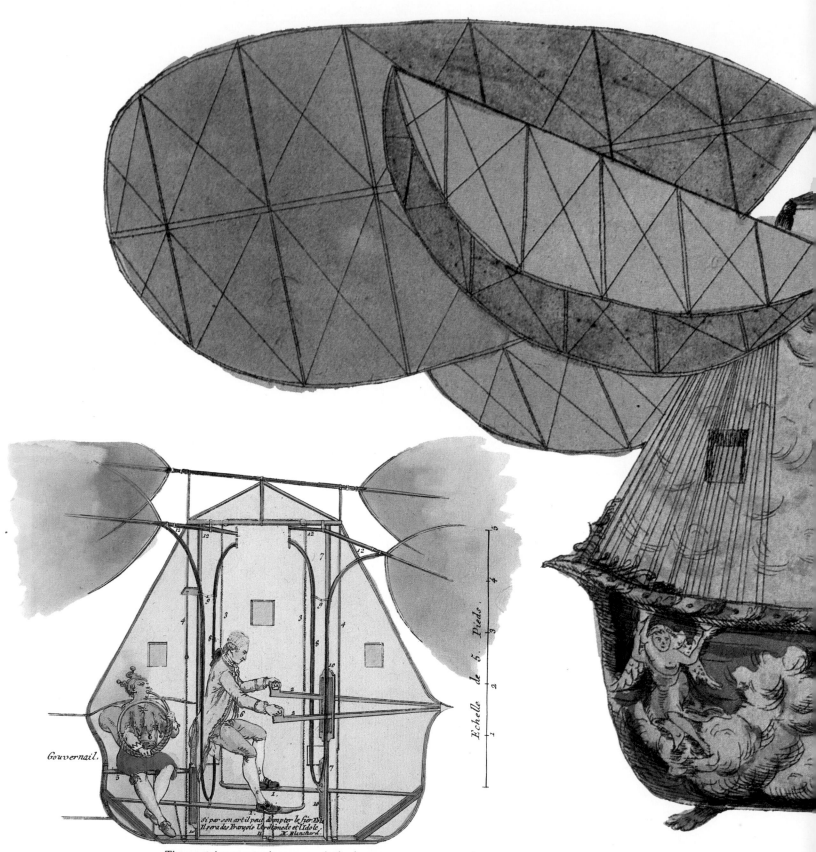

Gouvernail.

Si par son art il peut dompter le fier Bi.
Il sera des François l'archimede et l'idole.
J. Blanchard.

Echelle de 5 Pieds.

The partial cutaway above reveals the human power source of
Frenchman Jean Pierre Blanchard's 1781 Vaisseau Volant (Flying
Ship). In theory, the pilot worked pedals and levers to propel the
craft across the sky while a horn player offered musical inspiration.

Blanchard's flying machine, decorated in elegant rococo style, suggests a tented, winged bark. The vessel had a rudder for steering (right) and six flappers that, beating the air, were to supply lift and thrust. A shroud, painted with clouds, concealed the ship's inner workings—including the pilot and the musician.

*This fanciful engraving celebrates the alleged
18th Century flight of Joseph Patinho
and his so-called Flying Fish. The saw-nosed
fish—probably a hot-air balloon that
was rowed across the sky—reputedly soared
across a branch of the Tagus River,
from Plazentia to Coria, Spain, in 1784.*

CORIA

10

PLAZENTIA

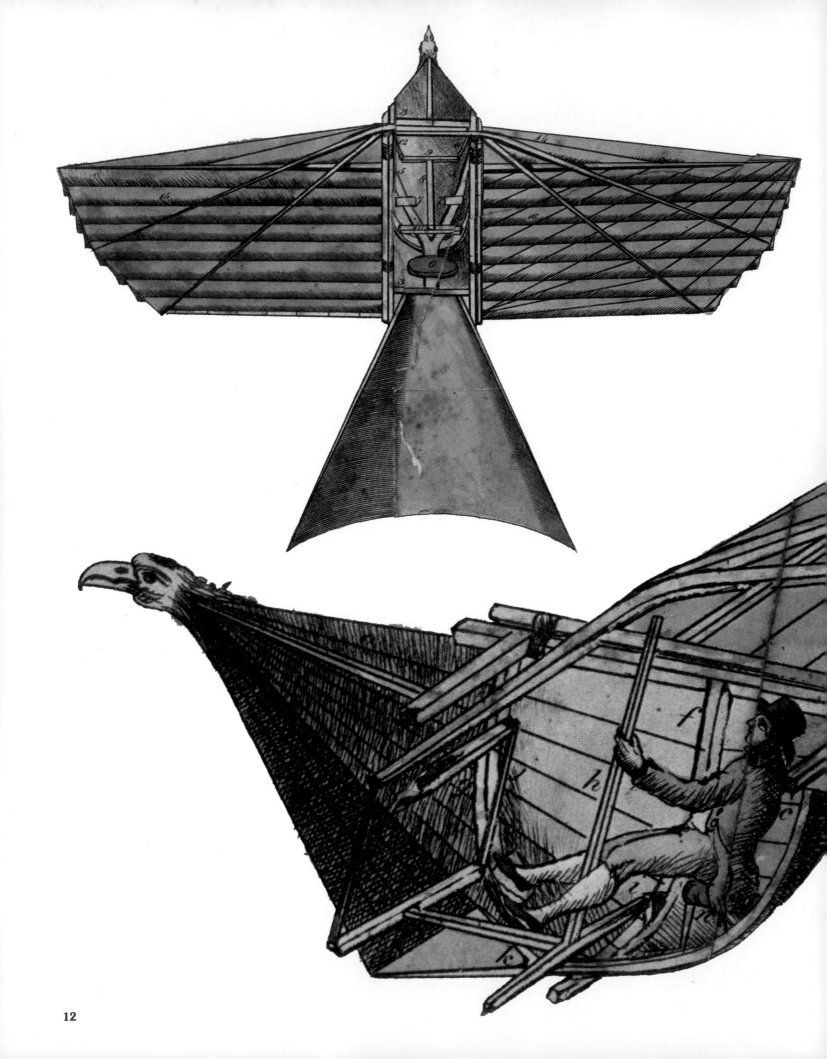

The illustration at left is a top view of the silk wings, fanlike tail and controls of an ornithopter envisioned—but never built—by 19th Century British inventor Thomas Walker. The cutaway below exposes the cockpit where, wrote Walker, "a man may sit and, by working a pair of wings with a lever, be able to ascend into the air and fly with as much safety and ease as a bird."

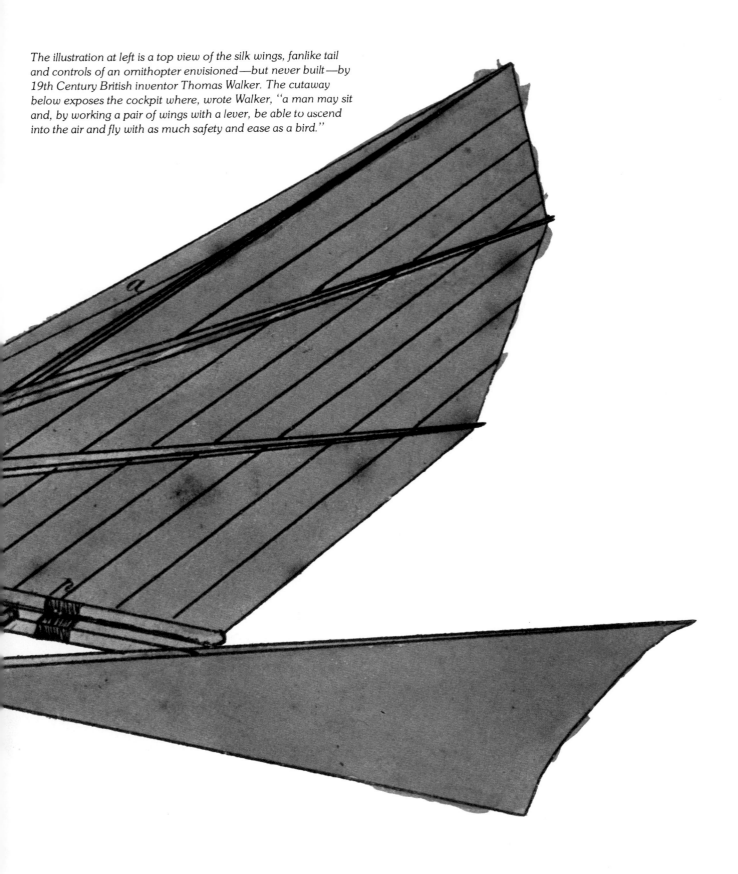

William Samuel Henson's remarkable Aerial Steam Carriage is pictured in imaginary flight over London in this engraving from the 1840s. Henson's brilliant concept—an early design for a propeller-driven, fixed-wing monoplane—is a prophetic suggestion of the modern airplane, though only a model of it was ever built.

1
In search of the "infinite highway"

The desire to fly," wrote Wilbur Wright, "is an idea handed down to us by our ancestors who, in their grueling travels across trackless lands in prehistoric times, looked enviously on the birds soaring freely through space, at full speed, above all obstacles, on the infinite highway of the air."

In the first years of the 20th Century, Wilbur Wright and his brother Orville tried repeatedly to take to that infinite highway. Repeatedly they failed. In August 1901, riding glumly back to Dayton, Ohio, from their latest trials at Kitty Hawk, North Carolina, Wilbur predicted that another thousand years might pass before men and women would be able to fly.

Thousands of years had already passed since man first dreamed of flight; the Wright brothers were merely among the latest, and by no means the best known, in a long procession of experimenters who had sought to fathom the mysteries of the air and fashion wings that would loft them above the earth. Clues to the secrets of flight had always been tantalizingly close at hand, suggested by the workings of the wind on drifting smoke or billowing sail, the course of an arrow, the wayward coasting of autumn leaves, and most teasingly by the effortless gliding of birds upon invisible currents. Even ancient man, observing these clues of nature, found that his imagination was fired.

From the beginning, some men did more than just dream. A host of early activists attempted to defy gravity by leaping from towers and high cliffs. Some covered themselves with feathers and flapped homemade wings; inevitably, they fell, breaking their legs or their skulls. Others draped themselves with billowing cloaks and tried to float upon the air. Foolhardy but courageous, they had nothing to support them but a consuming desire to fly, no models but the winged creatures—and not the slightest understanding of the principles of flight.

But their failures gave other men something to think about. Where had the wing flappers and tower jumpers gone wrong? Were their wings too small, their muscles too puny? Did flight require the support of a tail as well as wings? Gradually, the lessons of the pioneer jumpers— together with an expanding body of general scientific knowledge—led thoughtful men away from the idea of putting on wings. Instead, they turned to what seemed a more practical pursuit: designing vehicles that they hoped would carry man off the ground.

Even the most enlightened of these designers made false starts, trapped themselves in blind alleys of research or failed to follow the

Eilmer of Malmesbury, an English monk who was one of the first so-called tower jumpers, is memorialized in this stained-glass window in Malmesbury Abbey. Eilmer survived a floundering winged glide from the abbey's tower in the 11th Century.

17

Flight of the Foolish King

In ancient Persia, as in other early cultures, the heavens were regarded as the inviolable province of the gods. What happened when a legendary Persian monarch challenged that sacred tenet is told in the *Book of Kings,* written by the epic poet Ferdowsi about 1000 A.D.

According to the fable, King Kay Kavus, who was said to have ruled about 1500 B.C., was tempted by evil spirits to invade the heavenly realm in an ingenious but improbable flying craft. To a throne of wood and gold, wrote Ferdowsi, the King "attached long poles on which he tied legs of mutton." Four strong eagles who had been "fed unceasingly for a year and a month on fowls, roast meat and whole lambs" were lashed to the royal seat. When hunger struck, the eagles flapped frantically in an effort to reach the meat, carrying the chair and Kay Kavus aloft.

Predictably, the birds grew tired. Eagles, throne and king came to earth in a Chinese forest. There, humiliated and grief-stricken, Kavus was said to have "rested for a time devoting himself to adoration of the Creator." His fall was taken as a sign that man was not meant to fly, and Kay Kavus was known ever after as the Foolish King.

The brief flying folly of legendary Persian King Kay Kavus is illustrated in the two paintings at right. At top, in a 16th Century work, the King's ornate throne is borne aloft by four powerful eagles. In the miniature at bottom, probably from the 14th Century, the flight of the Foolish King comes to an ignominious end.

gleam of a practical idea. Leonardo da Vinci, the intellectual giant of the Renaissance, brought his brilliance to bear on the problem of mechanical flight, but he too clung to a misguided belief in flapping wings as a source of motive power. Sir George Cayley of England, who laid the foundations of modern aerodynamics early in the 19th Century, clearly envisioned a practical airplane—but he could not provide what he called a "prime mover," or suitable power plant. Clément Ader of France and Sir Hiram Maxim, the American-born British inventor, built powered machines that left the ground but could not truly fly; the distinguished American astronomer Samuel Langley constructed and tested a successful model, but his attempts to translate it into a flyable full-scale craft failed dismally. Hundreds of others wrestled with the challenge of heavier-than-air flight. Most found only disappointment, but an isolated few—among them Otto Lilienthal of Germany, Percy Pilcher of Scotland, Octave Chanute of the United States and Lawrence Hargrave of Australia—made valuable contributions to a steadily growing mass of aeronautical knowledge.

By the end of the 19th Century this accumulation of knowledge had created conditions that seemed to put flight at last within man's grasp.

It had never been science alone that beckoned men to the skies. Even the Wright brothers, whose coolheaded experiments with kites and gliders had by 1901 gained them a modest international reputation as aviation experts, were dedicated bird watchers, moved in part by the same ancient yearnings that had inspired the earliest dreams of human flight. But the earth, not the air, is man's natural environment and for centuries skeptics had warned that man's lack of wings was proof enough that he had no business trying to fly. Indeed, the oldest myths of human flight can be read as moral fables that warned of the disasters that awaited those who would defy the gods and attempt to invade the heavens above.

One of the most durable Greek myths tells of Daedalus and his son, Icarus, who sought to fly from imprisonment on the island of Crete with wings made of feathers held together by wax. All went well until Icarus ignored his father's warning and flew too close to the sun, "as if to reach heaven." The wax in the young man's wings melted, and Icarus plunged into the sea and drowned.

The earliest real-life birdmen were not deterred by such fables. There is no record of the first aerial pioneer who fitted himself with wings and leaped from a height down to earth; there were doubtless many such ventures before history began to identify these fledgling aviators. But one of the first recorded attempts occurred in the year 852 A.D., when the Moorish savant Armen Firman donned a voluminous cloak and bounded from a tower in Cordoba, Spain. If nothing else, Firman proved that a little knowledge can be dangerous, if not necessarily fatal. Assuming that his outspread garment would support him on a gliding flight through the air, he instead plummeted to earth. Fortunately, as his chronicler noted, "there was enough air in the folds of his cloak to prevent great injury when he reached the ground." Instead of flying, Firman had made a primitive parachute jump.

Moorish Spain was the scene of another attempted takeoff in about the year 875, when an Andalusian physician named Abbas ibn-Firnas ventured to display his flying skills to an appreciative audience on the ground. As one account told it, ibn-Firnas "covered himself with feathers for the purpose, attached a couple of wings to his body, and getting on an eminence, flung himself into the air, when, according to the testimony of several trustworthy writers who witnessed the performance, he flew to a considerable distance, as if he had been a bird."

So far, so good. But when the ambitious physician attempted to alight like a bird, he smashed heavily to the ground and severely injured his back. With more sympathy than understanding, the account explained that ibn-Firnas had crashed because, "not knowing that birds when they alight come down upon their tails, he forgot to provide himself with one."

The lack of a tail was blamed also for the near undoing of an 11th Century English monk named Eilmer, who fitted himself with wings and made a hopeful swoop from Malmesbury Abbey. A bewildered medieval historian reported years later that Eilmer "had by some means, I scarcely know what, fastened wings to his hands and feet so that, mistaking fable for truth, he might fly like Daedalus, and collecting the breeze on the summit of a tower, he flew for more than the distance of a furlong." Historians generally agree that Eilmer did indeed achieve some sort of uncontrolled glide, but if he managed to cover a furlong (an eighth of a mile) he could credit luck considerably more than skill. In any event, like ibn-Firnas, he had a rough landing. He fell hard to the ground, broke his legs and was crippled for life. "He himself used to say," the chronicler concluded, "that the cause of his failure was his forgetting to put a tail on the back part."

So far as is known, the first person to suggest an apparatus that might propel man through the air—and the first to commit to paper any scientific speculation about flight—was the celebrated English philosopher and scientist Roger Bacon, who lived from 1214 to 1292.

Bacon, a Franciscan monk, was a prolific writer with a deep interest in natural science, alchemy and mathematics. In about the year 1250 he wrote a book called *De Mirabili Potestate Artis et Naturae (Of the Marvelous Powers of Art and Nature)*, in which he sought to demonstrate the superiority of reason over the magical powers claimed by the alchemists of his day. Mankind, he said, was fully capable of building "instruments to fly" that would be propelled through the air by flapping, birdlike wings. Bacon even went on to make the cryptic claim that "there is an instrument to fly with, which I never saw, nor know any man that hath seen it, but I full well know by name the learned man who invented the same."

If such an invention existed, it was the best-kept secret of the 13th

An illumination from a 13th Century French manuscript includes one of the earliest known examples of a European windmill. Its horizontal spindle and vertical blades are suggestive of a modern propeller.

On the lap of the Madonna, a Christ child is shown holding a whirling toy in this panel painted by an unknown European artist around 1460. The string-pull toy prefigures the 20th Century helicopter.

Century, and Bacon, the only writer to mention the mysterious aircraft, never said another word about it. Nor did he inspire others to pursue his conception of a flying machine, for his observations on flight were not published for nearly 300 years. In any case, Bacon was off on the same wrong tack that many other men would take. The instrument he had suggested would later be called an ornithopter—a clumsy contrivance with artificial wings that invariably beat the air more in the manner of a barnyard hen than of a bird in flight.

The fact is that the workaday windmill, which was already in widespread use as a source of power throughout Europe, would ultimately be far more important than any wing-flapping apparatus in the development of powered flight. This useful aerodynamic tool foreshadowed the latter-day propeller, and by the 14th Century its simple airscrew principle was employed in the design of a popular child's toy that resembled a helicopter. Propeller-driven flying machines were still far in the future, however. Only the titanic Leonardo da Vinci foresaw that the airscrew might someday be used to lift men into the air; he envisioned a helicopter whose swiftly turning screwlike propeller "will make its spiral in the air and it will rise high."

Leonardo, the quintessential Renaissance man whose massive talents embraced art, music, architecture, mathematics, engineering and science, seemed at times to be almost obsessed with the notion of human flight. During the late 15th and early 16th Centuries he filled page after page of his voluminous notebooks with sketches of proposed flying machines and other aeronautical equipment—a body of work amounting to some 500 sketches and 35,000 words. But most of Leonardo's ideas were fatally flawed; except for the propeller-driven helicopter, the machines he designed were intended—like Roger Bacon's ornithopter—to be lifted and propelled by the flapping of their birdlike wings. Leonardo did improve on Bacon in one notable sense: His ornithopters, for all their lack of airworthiness, were drawn with stabilizing tail assemblies.

Despite his genius, Leonardo influenced the aeronautical thinking of his age no more than Bacon had. His research on the subject was not published until the late 1800s, and for more than a century after his death in 1519 human flight remained the province of rash birdmen with wings strapped to their bodies.

In 1499, even as Leonardo was filling his notebooks, his countryman Giovanni Battista Danti attempted a flight of sorts from a tower in Perugia. But one of his feathered wings malfunctioned, and as one account put it, Danti "fell heavily onto the roof of the church of St. Mary, and to his great distress, and to that of everyone, hurt his leg." A few years later, in 1507, an expatriate Italian known as John Damian equipped himself with wings of his own devising and flapped from the wall of Scotland's Stirling Castle. Damian's avowed destination was distant France, but he landed instead in a dunghill, where he broke his thigh bone. Damian, who was something of a charlatan, explained his crippling detour glibly enough: Among the feathers in his wings, he said, were those of a chicken, a creature whose plumage had a natural attraction to common soil. With wings made entirely of the feathers of eagles, he said, he could easily have made the flight to France. But he did not offer to try again.

Numerous other optimists fluttered in the plummeting wakes of Danti and Damian, and if they knew of their predecessors' mistakes, they failed to profit by them. Attempting to fly from the cathedral tower of Troyes, France, in 1536, an Italian clockmaker named Bolori flapped to his death on the pavement below. Some 70 years later yet another Italian airman, the artist Paolo Guidotti, took to the skies with wings fashioned of feathers on a whalebone frame; he fell to a rooftop and shattered his thigh. A French tightrope walker, watched expectantly by King Louis XIV, was seriously hurt during a winged leap in about 1660. And several years later a German named Bernoin died trying to fly in Frankfurt-am-Main.

Such ill-starred wing flappers made scant contribution to aeronautical knowledge or progress. But they did keep alive an interest in aviation, and by the mid-17th Century serious-minded men were beginning to turn their attention to flying machines. Among them were an Italian mathematician and two Englishmen—one a physicist, the other a clergyman. Together they would help change the way that men perceived the problem of human flight.

The Right Reverend John Wilkins, Bishop of Chester and founding member of the Royal Society of London for Improving Natural Knowledge, thought he understood why the intrepid birdmen continued to fall to the ground. Their main shortcoming, he wrote in 1648, was "want of experience, and too much fear, which must needs possess men in such dangerous and strange attempts." Anyone who aspired to winged flight, Wilkins advised, would do well to start practicing at an early age, taking one step at a time: "running on the ground, as an ostrich or tame goose will do, touching the earth with his toes; and so by degrees learn to rise higher, till he shall attain unto skill and confidence."

Wilkins' theories on aviation appeared in his book *Mathematical Magic,* which examined several methods by which flight "hath been or may be attempted." In addition to strap-on wings, he mentioned flight by spirits or angels, and human flight achieved with the assistance of birds—both of which he dismissed out of hand as being beyond the scope of mortals. He then went on to discuss what he called a "flying chariot," which he deemed "altogether as probable, and much more useful than any of the rest."

There was no imaginable invention, Wilkins said wisely, that "could prove of greater benefit to the world or glory to the author," and in speculating on what form such a craft might take, he seemed to grope toward some form of glider. Birds, he mused, can easily move

Renaissance Italy's fascination with flight is evoked in the winged figure on the frontispiece of this book, published in 1590, about the illustrious men of Bologna. The figure may have been inspired by the exploit of Giovanni Battista Danti, whose nearly fatal winged leap from a tower in 1499 had become a popular legend.

Seconds before his leap, Franz Reichelt unfolds his silken wings. Jauntily, he called out to those watching, "See you soon!"

Two newsreel frames record Reichelt's plunge. The fatal fall took five seconds.

A birdman's last jump

Amazingly, tower jumping continued—with results as tragic as ever—even after man discovered the secrets of powered flight. On February 4, 1912, a 33-year-old Austrian-born tailor named Franz Reichelt attempted a winged glide from one of the world's great landmarks, the Eiffel Tower in Paris.

Wearing a parachute-like suit that he hoped would enable him to float safely to earth, Reichelt climbed the stairs to the Tower's first platform—190 feet above the ground. He tossed a newspaper over the balustrade to test the winds, which were light. Then, climbing onto a chair atop a table, he spread his wings and jumped. The suit barely slowed his fall.

through the air with barely a beat of their wings, and thus it was not improbable that humans, "when all the due proportions in such an engine are found out," might someday be able to build a craft that would do likewise.

Wilkins never actually tried any of his rudimentary aeronautical precepts, but at least one of them turned out to be startlingly prescient: More than two centuries later, after following the same step-by-step procedure that Wilkins had prescribed for prospective birdmen, Germany's Otto Lilienthal made hundreds of successful glider flights. But Wilkins' greatest influence was on a young man of his own time, Robert Hooke, who determined—to his own satisfaction, at least—that arm-flapping human flight was impossible.

Robert Hooke was a prodigy who became a distinguished mathematician, physicist and inventor and was considered to be the finest mechanical engineer of his day. In 1655, when he was 20, he designed several flying-machine models and discussed them with Wilkins. During that same year, by Hooke's own account, he constructed "a module, which, by the help of springs and wings, raised and sustained itself in the air." If Hooke's machine, which was presumably an ornithopter, did indeed lift off the ground, it was probably the first such device ever to have done so.

Hooke's experiments and calculations at last led him to the firm, accurate—but for his time, revolutionary—conclusion that man's body does not possess the strength to power artificial wings, and that human flight would require some form of artificial propulsion. His disbelief in muscle power did not keep him from sharing the great interest of the scientific community in the reported flight of a French locksmith named Besnier. Hooke eventually presented a report on the locksmith's feat to the prestigious Royal Society, after reading about it in the *Journal des Sçavans,* a French publication that carried an account in its issue of December 12, 1678. This was the first known magazine story about an attempt at manned flight, and the first detailed description of an actual flying machine.

"This machine," explained the *Journal,* "consists of two rods, at each end of which there is an oblong frame of taffeta that folds from the top downward in the manner of folding window shutters. When one wishes to fly, one adjusts these rods onto the shoulders in such a way as to have two frames in front and two behind. The front frames are moved by the hands and the rear frames by the feet by pulling on a string that is attached to them." If the apparatus worked as planned, the alternating up-down actions of the hands and feet were intended to give the effect of walking on air.

Besnier's flight-training program indicates a possible familiarity with John Wilkins' step-by-step advice to would-be birdmen. "The inventor first flew down from a stool," the *Journal* account noted, "then from a table, afterward from a window, fairly high, and finally from a garret, from which he passed above the houses in the neighborhood."

The Right Reverend John Wilkins, Bishop of Chester, whose tautly reasoned writings stimulated interest in flying in the 1600s, was not without his flights of fancy. He suggested that contemporary birdmen operate wings with their legs—"which are naturally more strong" than arms—and thereby "walk or climb up into the air."

The 1678 flight of the French locksmith Besnier is memorialized by this wooden sign that hung outside an inn owned by a member of his family. Besnier's contraption employed both his arms and legs, purportedly enabling him to glide safely from a garret in the town of Sablé.

The story of Besnier's aeronautical accomplishments is of dubious accuracy. Most historians believe that the airborne locksmith probably made another rudimentary parachute jump. Whatever the truth, Besnier seems not to have attempted another demonstration of his flying skills. But in at least one respect the contemporary account of his feat sounded an authentic—and familiar—note. Besnier's ingenious contrivance was not more successful, reported the *Journal,* because it had no tail, "which would serve to support and to steer the person flying."

This lack of directional control would continue to be a critical stumbling block on the way to effective manned flight. The scientific investigators of a much later age, even after they had achieved sustained motion through the air, persistently overlooked the vital importance of flight control. Not until the Wright brothers' painstaking experiments at Kitty Hawk would that problem be confronted and solved.

While would-be fliers of Besnier's time were still trying to flap their muscle-powered wings, an Italian mathematician, physiologist and physicist named Giovanni Alfonso Borelli was doing his best to prove that the birdmen's most determined efforts were futile. In his treatise *De Motu Animalium (On the Movement of Living Things),* published posthumously in 1680, Borelli described the limitations of human physiology and demonstrated convincingly that man's muscle power is inadequate for lifting and propelling him in the manner of a bird, even if arm, chest and leg muscles are put simultaneously to the task. "It is impossible," he declared, "that men should be able to fly craftily, by their own strength."

Borelli was almost right; his judgment was not disproved for almost 300 years. In 1977 the Gossamer Condor, a lightweight aircraft driven by a pedal-powered propeller and supported by a 96-foot wingspan, flew for a little more than a mile. Two years later a similar craft, dubbed the Gossamer Albatross, was pedaled 23 miles across the English Channel by the same wiry pilot—who nearly collapsed at the end of his grueling flight.

But such man-powered aerial vehicles as the Condor and the Albatross were made possible only by a sophisticated technology that was totally beyond the grasp of earlier birdmen, and for a century after Borelli published his treatise, all but the most fanatic tower jumpers abided by his dampening conclusion. The search for lift and propulsion by means of some manner of man-operated winged device dwindled to an occasional brief plop, and man's attempts to fly seemed to be forever doomed to failure. A few scholars, however, believed that flight might be achieved by devices other than the flapping birdlike wings—although at least one of them had serious doubts about the ultimate wisdom of trying.

Francesco Lana de Terzi, an inventive Italian Jesuit of the 17th Century, suspected that a beneficent Providence would not permit the development of a flying machine, "by reason of the disturbance it would cause

Flawed concepts of a Renaissance giant

"There is in man," stated Leonardo da Vinci, the ability "to sustain himself in the air by the flapping of wings." From the early 1480s almost until his death in 1519, the great Renaissance man struggled to prove his assertion and thereby realize his vision of flight—what one biographer called "the most obsessing, most tyrannical of his dreams." Combining his knowledge of physics and mathematics with his observations of bird flight, Leonardo sketched a remarkable variety of muscle-powered ornithopters.

Impractical as his flapping-wing devices were, they at least hint at some features of modern aircraft, including the screwlike action of a helicopter's rotor.

A SELF-PORTRAIT OF LEONARDO IN 1514

Da Vinci's design of a four-winged ornithopter for a standing pilot is shown at right. The two sets of wings, which operated by pulleys and treadles, were to beat the air alternately, Leonardo wrote, "after the manner of the gait of a horse."

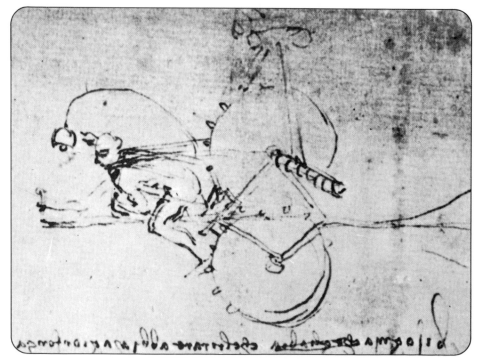

A da Vinci drawing from about 1485 details the gear train and transmission of a proposed flying machine. By manipulating hand levers and pedaling directly against the cogs of the lower wheel, the semiprone pilot was to power himself aloft. The bell-like device near the pilot's head is Leonardo's conception of an inclinometer.

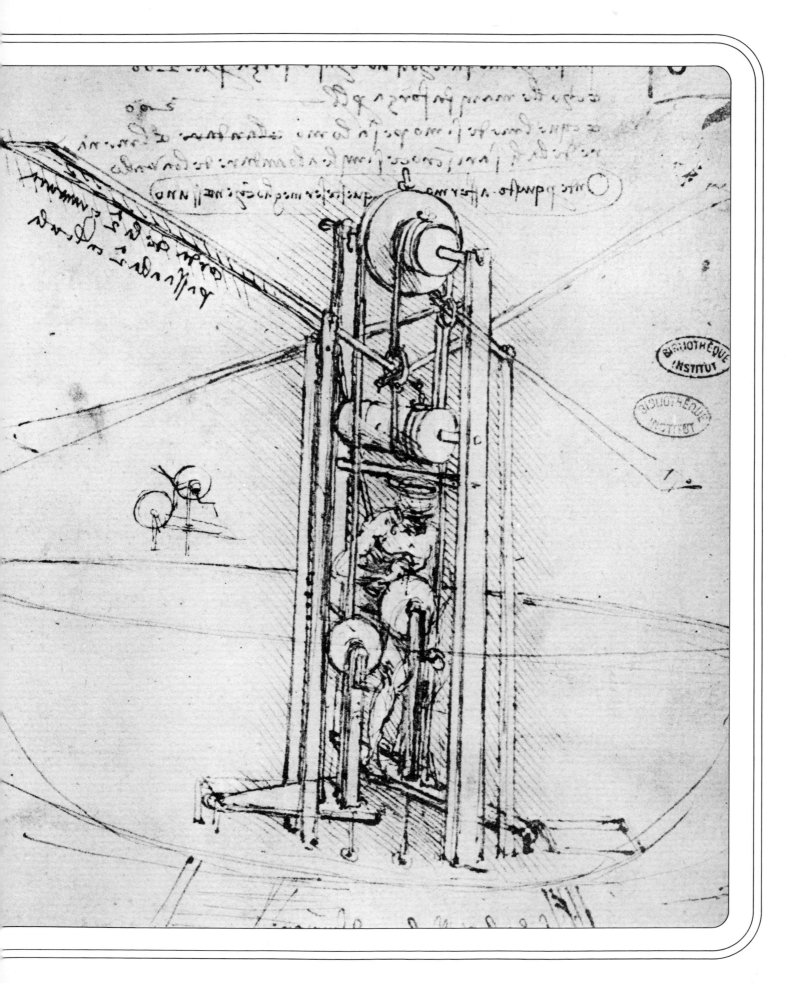

to the civil government of men." No city, ship or castle, Lana warned, could be safe from the depredations of rampaging aircraft hurling "fireworks and fireballs" on a hapless populace cowering below.

The imaginative priest was the first to foresee the terrors of aerial bombardment. Ironically, he was also the first to propose in detail a promising alternative to the cumbersome wings to which the diehard tower jumpers were so addicted.

After studying everything that was known in his day about atmospheric pressure and vacuums, Lana concluded that an airless container would be lighter than the air it displaced and would rise from the ground unless it was tied down. A container that was large enough and light enough, he reasoned, could lift some sort of flying boat along with it.

In 1670, Lana described and illustrated his proposed aerial vehicle in a widely read scientific article entitled "Prodromo dell' Arte Maestra" ("Introduction to the Master Art"). Four spheres of thin copper foil, each about 20 feet in diameter, were mounted above a boatlike craft designed to carry cargo and crew. When the globes were lightened by pumping out their enclosed air, Lana claimed, the entire apparatus would rise majestically into the sky. A sail attached to the vessel's mast would then catch the wind and move the flying boat through the ocean of the air.

For all his earnest studies, Lana did not perceive the most serious shortcoming in his proposal: Atmospheric pressure would have crushed his flimsy copper vacuum spheres. He also did not realize that his balloon-like globes would have needed no sail even if they did by some miracle become airborne. A balloon is its own sail, and no amount of billowing canvas will speed its progress through the air.

Flawed though it was, Lana's work represented the first scientific effort to design a lighter-than-air craft. He had, in fact, conceived the forerunner of the balloon, although it would be more than 100 years before the brothers Joseph and Étienne Montgolfier, who were well-educated papermakers from the French town of Annonay, achieved lighter-than-air flight.

The Montgolfiers had discovered that a paper bag filled with heated air will rise from the ground. After experimenting with increasingly larger bags made of silk, they staged a public launching of an enormous paper-lined linen balloon that rose to an altitude of 6,000 feet and drifted with the wind for about 10 minutes before touching down a mile away. Then, on the afternoon of November 21, 1783, two eager volunteers stepped into the basket of a gigantic Montgolfier balloon tied down in the Bois de Boulogne in Paris. Released from its moorings, the balloon ascended triumphantly into the atmosphere; the world's first human aeronauts, after drifting back and forth over Paris for some 25 minutes, dropped gently back to earth about five miles from their starting point.

Man's dream of bearing himself aloft had at last become a reality, and most flying enthusiasts were so captivated by balloons that for

Father Francesco Lana, the 17th Century Italian prophet of lighter-than-air flight, conceived a flying boat (left) that was novel enough but never would have flown. The paper-thin copper globes were supposed to lift the vessel after the air was pumped from them; in fact, they would have been crushed by atmospheric pressure.

a time the idea of winged flight lost much of its appeal. Scientists, adventurers and budding aeronautical experts turned their attention to lighter-than-air flight, which seemed to offer far more promise than putting on wings and floundering down into village squares or barnyard dung heaps.

And yet the balloonists had solved only one of manned flight's problems. Yes, they could lift themselves from the ground—though it took an immense balloon to bear even the lightest weight. But once airborne, they could only drift with the wind, unable to direct the course of their aerial travels. Until men could raise a craft that was heavier than air and then control its speed and direction, true and useful flight would remain beyond their grasp.

On a small and simple scale, such a device was already known in Europe, but its aeronautical significance had eluded the attention of balloonist and birdman alike. It was the kite, used in the Orient for almost 2,000 years and first observed by a European when the renowned traveler Marco Polo visited China during the last quarter of the 13th Century—not long after Roger Bacon had written of Western science's ability to devise "instruments to fly."

In his account of the remarkable things he had seen during his epic 24-year sojourn in Asia, Polo described the strange apparatus used by Chinese mariners to augur the chances of a successful sea journey. "When any ship must go on a voyage," he began, "the men of the ship will have a wicker framework, that is, a grate of switches, and to each

The wondrous mechanism that propels the birds

For all his envious watching, man failed for centuries to understand how birds fly. The basic misconception was that birds swim across the sky, propelled by a downward and backward wing stroke. In fact, as these drawings show, the wings move forward on the downstroke. A bird's forward thrust comes from the outer primary feathers of the wing tips, which serve as propellers.

As the downstroke begins, the tips of the primaries are bent and twisted upward at their trailing edges. In this position they bite into the air as an airplane's propeller does. The biting action impels the feathers forward, pulling with them the wing and hence the bird's body. On the upstroke, the primaries separate to allow a freer passage of the air, reducing drag. Then the cycle begins anew.

A sequence of drawings records the stroke cycle of a sea gull, from the start of the upstroke (left) to the end of the downstroke (right).

corner and side of that framework will be tied a cord, so that there are eight cords, and all of these are tied at the other end to a long rope. Next they will find some fool or drunkard and lash him to the frame, for no one in his right mind or with his wits about him would expose himself to that peril. Then they raise the framework into the teeth of the wind and the wind lifts up the framework and carries it aloft, and the men hold it by the long rope."

The framework was a kite; the fool or drunkard was secured to it either to serve as some form of talisman or to approximate the weight of the ship in relation to its sails. If the man-bearing kite shot skyward and stayed aloft, a safe and prosperous voyage was reckoned to lie ahead, and merchants rushed to get their goods aboard the departing vessel. A kite that failed to fly was taken as a sign of ill fortune (certainly for the witless passenger), and no one would entrust his life or merchandise to a ship so marked for potential disaster.

Marco Polo was impressed by the ingenuity of the Chinese in testing to see if the winds were favorable. But he was unaware of the deeper significance of what he had seen. The kite was a lightweight—but heavier-than-air—device that could lift a man into the air. To a limited extent, at least, it could be controlled by manipulating a set of cords. And even the simplest kite, one that a child could fly, carried solutions to many mysteries of aerodynamics.

Kites were generally unknown to Europeans in Marco Polo's time. But the Chinese had been flying them for more than a millennium, possibly since the Fourth or Fifth Century B.C., and their use spread to Japan soon thereafter. The earliest recorded kite flight of historic note took place in about 200 B.C., when the Chinese general Han Hsin dispatched a kite on a distance-measuring mission. By flying the kite over enemy fortifications and paying out a measured rope attached to it, the general was able to determine how far his engineers would have to dig in order to burrow under the enemy's walls.

For a thousand years thereafter, kites were used in China for aerial observation, as signaling devices and as playthings. At the siege of Nanking in the Sixth Century A.D., kites were used to signal information from the beleaguered city to army commanders in the field. By the 10th Century the Chinese were flying kites that had cambered, or curved, wings, which they had found more effective than flat-surfaced wings. Japanese kites, on the other hand, were large and flat, requiring tails for lift and balance.

Kites first appeared in Europe sometime after the 13th Century, probably by way of trade routes from the East, and were used primarily as military flags, and for decoration and entertainment. Not until the 18th Century did Western scientists turn to the kite as a tool for practical research. In 1749 a Scottish astronomer, Alexander Wilson, raised a series of kites that were carrying thermometers to measure air temperatures at various altitudes. Three years later the American Benja-

A good idea royally scorned

In 1764, Melchior Bauer, a 30-year-old inventor from the Germanic state of Saxony, traveled to England to ask King George III for £500 to build a flying machine he had designed. Bauer's concept was different from—and in one respect, more advanced than—the designs of his contemporaries, most of which featured flapping wings: His craft was to be lifted by a large, braced fixed wing with a dihedral set into it. Propulsion was to be supplied by a separate system of flappers, operated manually by the pilot.

The novelty of Bauer's design got him nowhere with King George or with another monarch he approached, Prussia's Frederick the Great. "A heavy affliction has disturbed thy brain," a scornful counselor to Frederick is said to have told him. Branded a fool, Bauer abandoned his project. But history vindicated him: Fixed, dihedrally set wings became standard components of modern airplanes.

Captioned in his own hand, these original drawings by Melchior Bauer detail his flying machine. At right, a side view shows the craft's source of thrust: a series of shutter-like flappers. Below, a front view reveals its fixed, dihedrally set wing.

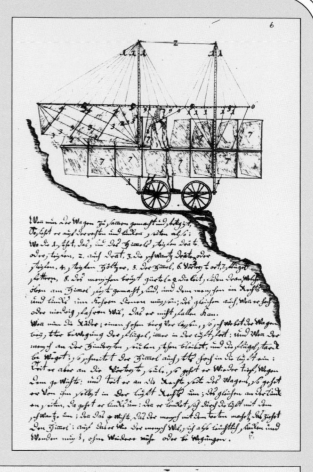

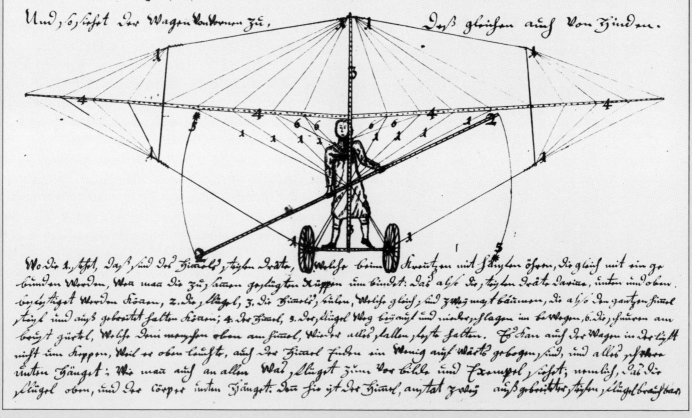

min Franklin flew a kite during a thunderstorm to demonstrate the electrical nature of lightning; Franklin's friend and fellow scientist, Joseph Priestley, observed that the wire cord of the kite "collected electric fire very copiously."

Aerial research with the unwieldy kites of Wilson and Franklin's day was not intended to aid in the long-sought conquest of the air. Yet many inquisitive men must have guessed that the study of wind-borne kites might help unlock the secrets of winged flight. One of those who did was the Englishman George Cayley.

Only 10 years old when the first manned balloon rose into the sky in 1783, Cayley dreamed as a boy of the wonders of balloon flight. But he spent a lifetime seeking to develop a heavier-than-air vehicle supported by wings modeled after the basic form of the ancient kite. He knew that the devotion of more lives than his would be required before that quest was ended, and that many a bold pioneer might perish on the way to achieving safe and effective human flight. But he realized, too, that he had embarked on an epic mission for the benefit of all mankind. "I am well convinced," he wrote in 1804, "that Aerial Navigation will form a most prominent feature in the progress of civilization." ～～

The Chinese origins of the kite—man's earliest heavier-than-air flying device—are acknowledged in this engraving from the 1840s, printed in an English book about China. Until the 19th Century, Western man was unaware that in the rigid wing of the kite lay one of the secrets of flight.

A skyful of curiosities

The advent of the Industrial Revolution marked a time when any sort of mechanical progress seemed possible, and imaginative men nurtured fresh dreams of human flight. Kites and balloons had been shown capable of lifting men—even one on horseback—and the adaptation of steam engines to drive ships and railway locomotives early in the 19th Century inspired proposals for their use in a multitude of other ways, including powered flight.

Most of the ideas were beyond reach or reason—then or ever. But some of the contraptions they spawned were actually built and a few of them contained the germs of practical technology.

All this was fertile ground for satire. The engraving at right and the one on the following pages, both published in London in 1829, are by William Heath, one of the era's most popular caricaturists. They were aimed at what was called the "March of Intellect"—a phrase applied sardonically to most aspects of progress, from improving the lot of the lower classes to the latest scientific marvel. Outlandish airborne conveyances and elaborate steam-powered machines were among the satirists' favorite subjects, both for the unlikelihood of their ever working and for the social upheaval it was feared they would cause if they did.

Flying curiosities fill the sky in this satirical English engraving: Cavalry approaches on winged horses shod with balloons, an "aerial ship" is steered by enormous paddles, a mounted huntsman dangles from a balloon, and a man-carrying kite tows a ship. In a cutaway house, steam-powered devices do the chores, while in the foreground three ragged workmen, presumably liberated from such labors by similar machinery, discuss the merits of London's fashionable eating places.

Steam power, ambitious construction projects and flight are the targets of this 1829 Heath print. A Grand Vacuum Tube connects London and the Indian region of Bengal. Steam horses and wagons clutter the London streets, where a winged postman (lower left) delivers the mail. In the sky, castles are built on clouds, a batlike ornithopter carries convicts to Australia, balloons transport troops and a fashionably dressed woman rides behind a kite.

2

The scientific visionaries

Sir George Cayley's coachman eyed the winged contraption on the hilltop with the apprehension of a man who felt more at ease with horses than with machines. He had seen several such exotic vehicles during his service with Sir George, but he had hardly expected that his 80-year-old employer would ever ask him to ride in one of them. Yet now, under his master's watchful eye and with the entire household of Brompton Hall looking on, he gamely climbed aboard.

The machine rolled forward on its tricycle undercarriage and the coachman found himself hurtling swiftly down the slope toward a narrow valley. The ground seemed to drop away beneath him and he was alone in the sky, crouching in a boatlike shell suspended from a billowing set of cloth wings.

From the far side of the valley, another low hill seemed to advance on the coachman with frightening speed. The strange craft dipped, leveled out and jounced to a landing on the slope. Excited onlookers rushed to the scene as the shaken coachman pulled himself free and blurted out, "Please, Sir George, I wish to give notice. I was hired to drive, not to fly!"

Cayley's granddaughter, who recounted this picturesque incident years later, was a child at the time, and hers is the only eyewitness report. But evidence pieced together from her grandfather's notebooks suggests that the event took place much as she described it, and that Cayley's coachman had made the world's first manned flight in a fixed-wing glider.

The year was 1853, and as George Cayley entered his eighties, he was still pursuing a vision of controlled human flight in a heavier-than-air craft. Success continued to elude him, but Cayley's faith was unfailing. He still believed, as he had written as early as 1809, in the fantastic notion that men would soon transport passengers and freight "more securely by air than by water, and with a velocity of from 20 to 100 miles per hour."

Cayley was virtually alone in his boundless optimism. To be sure, the early 19th Century was a golden age of scientific inquiry. But the onrushing Industrial Revolution demanded practical knowledge that could be applied to the immediate needs of commerce and industry. Canals, bridges, machinery, steamships and railways were matters of solid, useful concern, worthy of the attention of serious men; only dilettantes

More than anyone else, the 19th Century Yorkshire baronet Sir George Cayley was responsible for turning the pursuit of flight from an amusement into a science. He formulated the basic principles of heavier than air flight and in 1853 built the first successful man-carrying glider.

dabbled in such dubious enterprises as trying to fly. Cayley was the exception. An extraordinarily gifted aeronautical pioneer, he conceived and built the first airplane of modern configuration, and prepared the way for all subsequent achievements in aviation.

George Cayley was born in Yorkshire in 1773 and grew up on the family estate at Brompton. He showed an early interest in mechanical matters, and as a teenager he began to haunt the village watchmaker's shop to learn the intricate workings of gears, wheels and springs. Encouraged by his mother, he began keeping a journal to record his observations and to make sketches of the plant and animal life of the countryside. As his youth and young manhood went by, an odd assortment of entries appeared in the journal: a recipe for ginger beer, for example, and speculation on how much strength an insect might require to climb over a blade of grass. Cayley kept detailed notebooks for the rest of his life, leaving a revealing portrait of a man whose interests ranged from charting the rate of growth of his thumbnail to measuring the exact timing of a crow's downward wingbeat.

News of the Montgolfier brothers' balloon ascents in 1783 stimulated Cayley's youthful interest in human flight. But, with typical independence of spirit, he was not swept up by the balloon mania that gripped much of Europe; instead, he developed an intense preoccupation with the flight of birds, and with ways its principles might be adapted by men. Fortunately, his parents were in a position to provide him with the kind of education that could further broaden his inquiring mind, and at the age of 17 he was sent to Nottingham to be one of four young people tutored by the Reverend George Walker, a brilliant scholar and Fellow of the Royal Society.

Already adept in mathematics and eager to learn more about everything else, Cayley advanced quickly under Walker's guidance. His competitive spirit was sharpened by the brilliance of his three fellow students, one of whom was Walker's only daughter, Sarah. Spoiled from infancy by her widowed father, Sarah would fly into fierce rages if her every whim was not satisfied. But she was attracted by young Cayley, and in his presence she managed some control over her tantrums; George, in turn, was smitten by Sarah. In 1795, three years after inheriting the family title and estates, Sir George Cayley, at the age of 22, married Sarah and installed her in Brompton Hall.

The Cayley household was hardly a model of domestic bliss. Sarah showed no interest in her husband's scientific concerns, and her temper grew alarmingly worse; at times she seemed to have lost her mind completely. More and more, Cayley took refuge from his wife's rages by withdrawing to his work shed in the Low Garden of the Brompton estates, where he pursued his aeronautical experiments and other mechanical interests.

In 1796, within a year of his marriage, Cayley made his first practical experiment in heavier-than-air flight when he built a small helicopter

This sketch of a fixed-wing glider, engraved by young George Cayley on a silver disk in 1799, is the first depiction of an airplane of modern configuration, with separate systems for lift, propulsion and control. The pilot's cockpit is below the wing.

Cayley drew this rough sketch of the kite-winged glider he constructed in 1804. About four feet in length, the glider was the world's first flyable model aircraft.

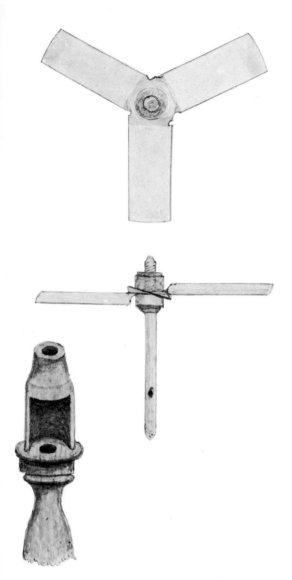

Cayley's interest in flight encompassed even the simple flying top, a popular child's toy. He made these drawings of his improved version of the toy (top and side views) and its launching base in 1855 when he was 81, noting with pride that his model would "mount upwards of 90 feet into the air." An obvious forerunner of the helicopter rotor, Cayley's top was also, as he observed, a "beautiful specimen of the action of the screw propeller."

model, based on a toy flying top from China. Cayley impaled two corks on opposite ends of a short shaft and equipped each cork with a set of four feathers inclined in opposite directions. He powered his miniature flying machine with a simple whalebone bow-and-string mechanism attached to the shaft. When the bowstring was wound around the shaft and then permitted to unwind, the little feather propellers lifted the model to the ceiling.

Cayley had thus applied the concept of the airscrew to mechanical flight. But having done so, he neglected it for most of the rest of his life. Not until almost 60 years later did he make a larger and more sophisticated helicopter model with a single three-bladed metal rotor.

Long before then, however, the baronet had envisioned a fixed-wing craft he deemed so epochal that in 1799 he engraved the design on both sides of a tiny silver disk to preserve it for posterity. One side of the disk shows a fixed-wing glider with its wings—apparently made of cloth—stretched between two spars, a boat-shaped fuselage in which the pilot is seated, and a tail unit for vertical and horizontal control. The other side of the disk illustrates the forces of lift, drag and thrust acting upon a wing form.

Cayley's design, which he detailed in a set of annotated drawings, had its weaknesses. For one, a paddle unit intended to propel the craft through the air would have been completely useless. For another, the wing was not truly arched, like a bird's wing; its curvature came from air pressure that billowed the cloth stretched between two poles. But the concept had its strengths as well. Cayley understood the separate functions of lift, control and propulsion, which earlier pioneers had failed to comprehend, and the craft, if he had built it, would have had a basically modern configuration.

At this stage, the young baronet's ideas on bird propulsion were scarcely more advanced than those of Leonardo da Vinci, three centuries earlier. But during the few years that followed, as Cayley continued to scrutinize gliding birds, observing the curvature of their wings and measuring their weight, body surface and velocity, he came to understand a good deal about the aerodynamics of the flight of birds, including the propeller-like function performed by the wing tips. In this, as in many other aspects of his aeronautical work, he was nearly 100 years ahead of his time.

Cayley applied to his specialized investigations a number of concepts and mechanisms employed in other fields. One device that he appropriated was a whirling-arm apparatus previously used in studying the effects of air resistance on projectiles and windmill sails. He built such a device of his own, powered by a weighted cord dropped over a pulley and down a stairwell, on the upper landing of Brompton Hall, prudently waiting for an occasion in the fall of 1804 when his stormy-tempered wife was away from home. To one end of the arm, which was designed to spin horizontally as well as to lift vertically, Cayley attached a foot-square airfoil, or wing; to the other end he attached small weights. He

Cross-country by kite power

The first controllable airborne device actually to transport people to a chosen destination was the simple kite. In 1827 an English schoolmaster named George Pocock, who had built kites that were buoyant enough to lift his children off the ground, harnessed a pair of kites to a lightweight carriage and drove the 40 miles from Bristol to Marlborough "at the amazing rate of 20 miles per hour." There was "no plunging, no sudden jerks," Pocock reported; because the weight of the carriage was partly supported by the kites, it fairly skimmed over the uneven road.

Pocock called his kite-driven vehicle a Char-volant (from "chariot" and *"cerf volant,"* the French term for kite), and the next year he demonstrated it before King George IV at the Ascot races. He also published an amusingly bombastic account of his early experiments under the title "The Aeropleustic Art or Navigation in the Air," in which he took pains to explain how his Char-volant could make headway not only with a following wind but in a cross wind by using guide ropes to angle the kites. Furthermore, he asserted, "where there is space for traverse, as on plains or downs, it is possible to beat up against the wind"—in effect, tacking like a sailboat.

To provide for every eventuality, however, Pocock suggested that the Char-volant might tow a wheeled platform carrying a pony; if the winds proved altogether uncooperative, the pony could supply the motive power.

Latin and Greek inscriptions, swirling calligraphy and a quote from Milton embellish the title page of George Pocock's grandiloquent little book, published in 1827, in which he extolled the advantages of traveling by kite power.

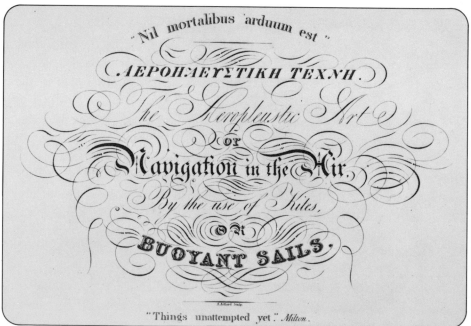

By "harnessing the invincible winds," kite-drawn carriages move in three directions on the same breeze in an engraving from Pocock's book.

then noted how much weight was lifted when the wing was whirled through the air at various speeds and angles.

Later, Cayley elaborated on these experiments to test the lifting power of larger airfoils and the effects of streamlining, thus obtaining valuable information about air resistance that he subsequently applied to full-sized wings. Yet he was not altogether satisfied with testing surfaces in a circular motion. In the same notebook entry that records his first whirling-arm experiment, Cayley describes his efforts to determine how an airfoil would perform if it moved forward in a straight line. And in reaching for such a form, Cayley designed and flew the first true aircraft model in history.

This pioneering model was small and deceptively simple: The main plane, or wing form, was a common paper kite set at a six-degree angle on the forward portion of a slender wooden pole. The rear of the pole supported a cruciform tail assembly—providing both horizontal and vertical control—attached by a universal joint so that it could be set at any angle. A movable weight could be positioned anywhere along the underside of the rod to vary the center of gravity and to keep the model in level flight.

Cayley was rightly pleased with his kite-plane; watching it fly he seemed to catch a glimpse of wondrous things to come. "It was very pretty to see it sail down a steep hill," he wrote, "and it gave the idea that a larger instrument would be a better and safer conveyance down the Alps than even the sure-footed mule, let him meditate his track ever so

An illustration of Cayley's design for two huge motorized airships, published in 1817, shows an end view (left) of an oval hydrogen-filled balloon propelled by what Cayley called rotary flyers, and a side view of a similar ship with flappers—a propulsion system that Cayley misguidedly preferred. The propellers and the flappers were to be driven by engines housed in the cars suspended from the balloons. A passenger in the car at left dangles a small parachute over the side.

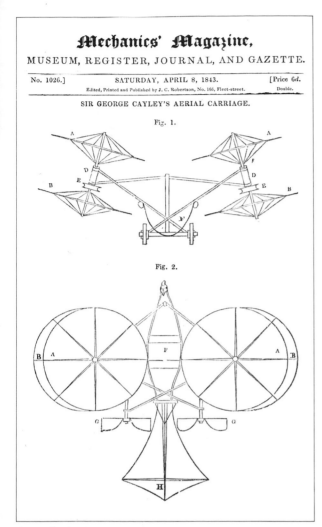

Mechanics' Magazine,

MUSEUM, REGISTER, JOURNAL, AND GAZETTE.

No. 1026.]   SATURDAY, APRIL 8, 1843.   [Price 6d.

Edited, Printed and Published by J. C. Robertson, No. 166, Fleet-street.   Double.

SIR GEORGE CAYLEY'S AERIAL CARRIAGE.

Fig. 1.

Fig. 2.

Cayley's idea for a convertiplane is illustrated in top and front views on the frontispiece of Mechanics' Magazine in 1843. The craft was to be lifted to a safe altitude by two pairs of helicopter-like rotors, then the rotor blades were to flatten out to form four umbrella-like wings that would support the craft as it was propelled horizontally by two pusher airscrews.

intensely. The least inclination of the tail toward the right or left made it shape its course like a ship by the rudder.''

This was the first known use of the kite's aerodynamic principles in the construction of a glider; Cayley would go on to use the kite form repeatedly, both in models and in full-sized craft.

Sir George crowded innumerable pursuits into the five years following his first model-plane flight: He experimented with finned projectiles, designed a lightweight aircraft wheel, and developed a hot-air engine—which was not, unfortunately, the light ''prime mover'' that he had said he needed for aeronautical purposes. Then in 1809 he topped his earlier achievement by building a full-sized glider with which an assistant was able to make some very tentative hops into the air.

Cayley did not describe this pioneering machine in his notebooks, but he twice referred to it in a landmark article, ''On Aerial Navigation,'' published in three parts in *Nicholson's Journal of Natural Philosophy, Chemistry and the Arts* in 1809 and 1810. The glider had a wing surface of 300 square feet, he wrote, and he claimed that ''its steerage and steadiness were perfectly proved, and it would sail obliquely downward in any direction, according to the set of the rudder. Even in this state, when any person ran forward in it, with his full speed, taking advantage of a gentle breeze in front, it would bear upward so strongly as scarcely to allow him to touch the ground; and would frequently lift him up, and convey him several yards together.''

Although he knew that the scientific world was disinclined to deal seriously with the idea of flight, Cayley had submitted his lengthy article to *Nicholson's Journal* in response to reports that one Jacob Degen, a Viennese watchmaker, had lofted himself into the air with a pair of umbrella-shaped wings. These reports proved false—Degen had actually been lifted by a balloon—but Cayley believed them. Perhaps by publishing his observations he sought to gain recognition for his own achievements in aeronautics. In any case, as he explained in a letter to a fellow enthusiast, he chose to use the term ''aerial navigation'' in his discussion of flying, ''for the sake of giving a little more dignity to a subject rather ludicrous in the public's estimation.''

Cayley himself saw nothing ludicrous about flying and noted at the beginning of his article that his findings could well hasten ''the attainment of an object that will in time be found of great importance to mankind; so much so, that a new era in society will commence, from the moment that aerial navigation is familiarly realized.'' And he expressed the fond hope that England would excel its Continental rivals in aeronautical research. Competition to bring about the age of flying machines, he wrote—five years before Waterloo—was ''a more worthy contest than that of arms.''

The article got right to the crux of the challenge facing aeronautical investigators. ''The whole problem,'' Cayley wrote, ''is confined within these limits—to make a surface support a given weight by the application of power to the resistance of air.'' Then, for the first time anywhere,

45

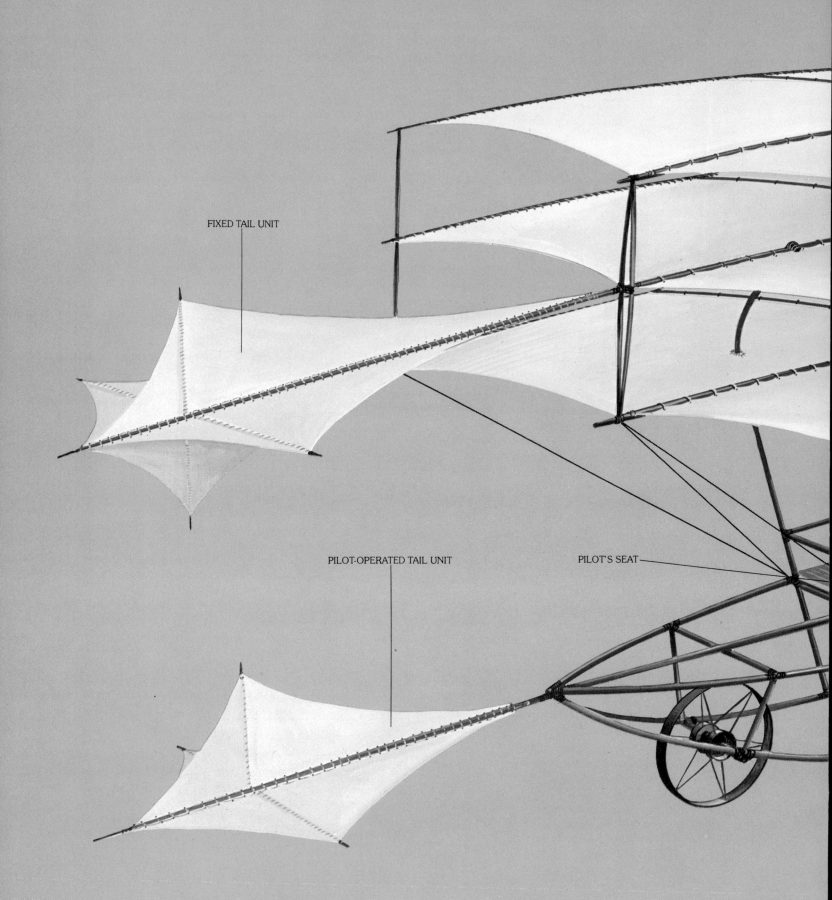

FIXED TAIL UNIT

PILOT-OPERATED TAIL UNIT

PILOT'S SEAT

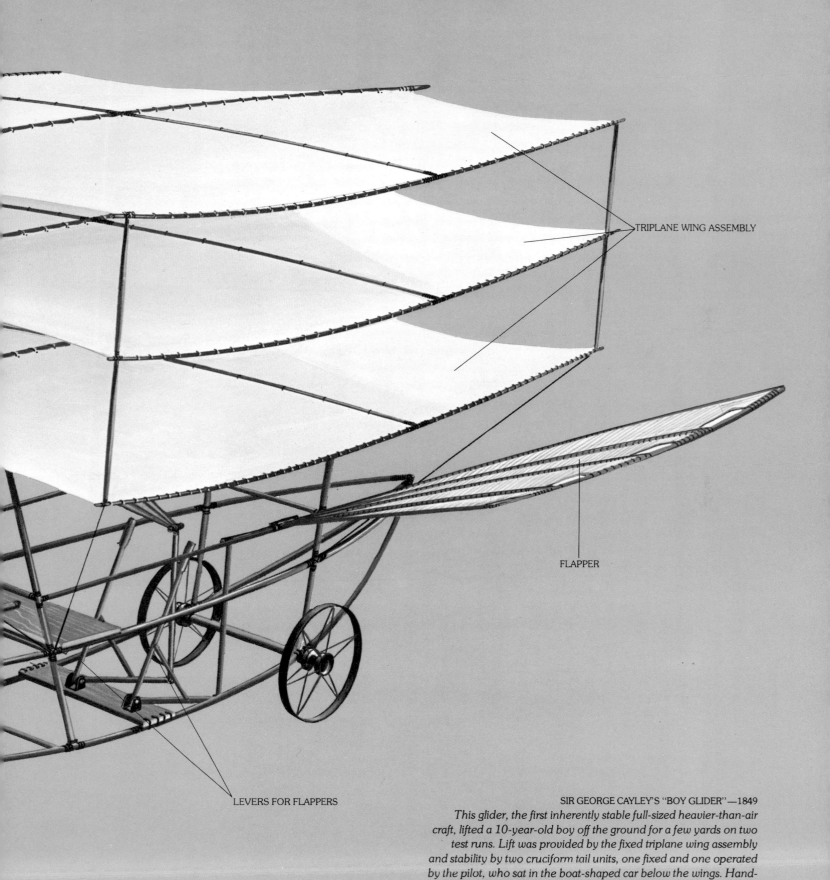

TRIPLANE WING ASSEMBLY

FLAPPER

LEVERS FOR FLAPPERS

SIR GEORGE CAYLEY'S "BOY GLIDER"—1849
This glider, the first inherently stable full-sized heavier-than-air craft, lifted a 10-year-old boy off the ground for a few yards on two test runs. Lift was provided by the fixed triplane wing assembly and stability by two cruciform tail units, one fixed and one operated by the pilot, who sat in the boat-shaped car below the wings. Hand-pumped flappers were to propel the glider once it was in the air.

Cayley spelled out the principles and practical applications of aero-dynamics. In minute and illuminating detail, he explained his theories, described his practical work and suggested avenues that might be followed by other experimenters. His paper provided signposts for all future research and development in aviation.

But Cayley had underestimated his readers' skepticism and indifference. His brilliant paper should have caused a revolution in scientific thinking, but it created barely a ripple. Most of Cayley's contemporaries were simply not ready for serious consideration of flight—three times during the next 30 years he tried to form an aeronautical society, but he could drum up little interest. Yet his experiments had brought him a small measure of fame, and they attracted the attention of a few students of flight—among them a fellow countryman named William Samuel Henson. Inspired by Cayley's research, Henson used it as a basis for his own work, and developed one of the most remarkable and influential airplane designs of the era.

Like Cayley, Henson had wide-ranging inventive talents. Born in 1812, he followed his father into the lacemaking industry in Somerset, but he also worked at developing a breech-loading cannon, an ice-making machine and a method for waterproofing fabrics; he took out patents for a safety razor, for lacemaking machinery and for improvements in steam engines.

By about 1840, Henson had turned his attention to aeronautics; three years later he patented and published a design for what he called an "Aerial Steam Carriage," suggesting that the craft might well be used "for conveying letters, goods and passengers from place to place."

Henson's aerial carriage existed only in the colorful and detailed drawings that he submitted with his patent application, but the design was a brilliant preview of the modern airplane. The drawings showed a graceful monoplane with a wingspan of 150 feet, the fixed wings cambered for lift and braced with ribs and spars. The tail unit combined the control functions of elevator and rudder. Two six-bladed pusher airscrews—or rear propellers—were to be driven by a 25- to 30-horsepower steam engine set in a fuselage equipped with a tricycle undercarriage.

Sketchy rumors of the Henson design had circulated for months before the details appeared in the April 1, 1843, issue of *Mechanics' Magazine*. Although the magazine's editor observed that the proposed craft closely followed the aeronautical principles laid down by Sir George Cayley, the same issue carried a letter in which Cayley cast doubt on a basic element of the Henson design: The steam engine, he said, was far too heavy for aerial navigation.

The next week's issue of *Mechanics' Magazine* carried more commentary by Cayley, who upon further study had discovered yet another basic flaw in Henson's project. The very size of the vehicle, he wrote, would doom it to failure, for air turbulence would exert such leverage

Pioneer parachutist Robert Cocking is shown ascending beneath a balloon (left) and in three stages of his calamitous descent (right).

ROBERT COCKING

Rise and fall of a balloon-borne parachutist

In his landmark treatise, "On Aerial Navigation," Sir George Cayley discussed the 1802 parachute jump of André Jacques Garnerin—the first ever made in England. During Garnerin's descent his umbrella-shaped chute had swayed violently from side to side, and Cayley, after some experimentation, concluded that an inverted cone would make a much more stable parachute.

One of the spectators at Garnerin's jump was the painter Robert Cocking. Already a balloon enthusiast, Cocking became intrigued with parachutes and tried to improve on Garnerin's umbrella design. With the publication of Cayley's article in 1810, Cocking had the design he was looking for; he experimented with small inverted cone-shaped models, but not until 1837, when he was 61, was he able to make the jump he had been dreaming of.

Cocking proposed to the owners of a successful new balloon, the *Royal Nassau,* that they pay for the building of a parachute of his design; in return he would provide a

spectacular show by jumping from their balloon. They agreed, and the parachute was built; shaped like a shallow funnel, it was 33 feet in diameter and weighed 223 pounds, 10 times the weight of a modern chute. Cocking was to ride in a basket beneath the mouth of the funnel.

Posters all over London publicized the forthcoming jump; construction of the chute was barely finished by the appointed day and it was never tested with a dead weight. Cocking, however, appeared confident. The balloon lifting the parachute rose to 5,000 feet; Cocking bade farewell to the balloonists and yanked a release, freeing the chute. For a few seconds it floated steadily downward as he had hoped, but then the funnel began to collapse and Cocking plummeted earthward beneath a fluttering mass of fabric and struts. Later tests showed that structural weakness, not Cayley's design, had been the cause of the failure, but that was no consolation to Cocking: He died within minutes of hitting the ground.

on the huge wing surface that the wings would be ripped apart in flight.

But Cayley had a solution to this problem, and it was a brilliant departure from his previous work in aeronautics. Wings to lift and sustain great weights in the air, he wrote, "ought not to be made in one plane but in parallel planes one above the other at a convenient distance." Such an arrangement, he explained, would reduce the likelihood of damage to a large single wing without sacrificing the required wing surface. He went on to propose wings in "the form of a *three decker*"—the italics are his—"each deck being eight or 10 feet from the other, to give free room for the passage of the air between them."

In time, the multiwing notion first suggested by Cayley would be adopted by a host of other aviation pioneers, Wilbur and Orville Wright among them. But Henson ignored Cayley's advice and stuck with a single-wing design for his proposed aerial steam carriage. Lacking funds to build a prototype, he and his associate, John Stringfellow, proceeded with a grandiose scheme for launching an international airline, the Aerial Transit Company, for which they attempted to raise funds with a massive barrage of publicity. Descriptions and illustrations of the proposed craft appeared in such popular journals as *The Illustrated London News* and *L'Illustration* of Paris. Fanciful scenes were reproduced not only in magazines but on souvenir items such as decorative cloths and handkerchiefs, showing the aerial carriage steaming over London, the English Channel, the exotic "Plains of Hindustan," the coast of France, the Pyramids and even faraway China.

Claims for the craft were so grandiose, and the promotion so lavish, that interest turned to skepticism and then to ridicule. Potential backers of Henson's scheme withdrew their support in the face of jeers and laughter, and the Aerial Transit Company died an early death.

Scarcely discouraged, Henson and Stringfellow set out to build and test a scale model of their flying machine, hoping for results impressive enough to attract funds for a full-sized craft. The experiments seemed promising but support was not forthcoming, and in September 1846, William Henson appealed to Cayley for help. "We feel very sanguine as to the result of our endeavour," he wrote, "and consider that we have arrived at that stage of proceedings which justifies us in obtaining that pecuniary assistance necessary to carry on our efforts upon an enlarged scale and with increased energy. We therefore resolved to apply to you as the Father of Aerial Navigation to ascertain whether you would like to have anything to do in the matter or not."

Cayley's reply was gracious enough, and he surely must have relished being addressed as the Father of Aerial Navigation. "I had thought that you had abandoned the subject," he wrote, "which tho' true in principle, you had rushed upon with far too great confidence as to its practice some years ago. If you have been making experiments since that time you will have found how many difficulties you have to adjust and overcome before the results you wish can be accomplished." Cayley concluded that, while he approved of Henson's zeal, he could spare

William Samuel Henson was an engineer in England's lacemaking industry before he turned his hand to aircraft design in the 1840s. His proposed Aerial Steam Carriage was the first design to call for the use of airscrews to drive a fixed-wing monoplane.

John Stringfellow was Henson's colleague in the lace trade and in aeronautical projects. He helped develop a lightweight steam engine for the Aerial Steam Carriage and persisted in vain efforts to build a model of it that would fly.

no money to support his experiments. Of course, he added, he would be most gratified if Henson could show some proof of progress in achieving mechanical flight—in which case, Cayley said he "perhaps might be able to aid you in some manner by my experience in connexion with other mechanical persons."

Henson, evidently, was more interested in funding than in moral support, and he proceeded without further correspondence with Cayley. In 1847 Henson and Stringfellow conducted final tests with a miniature aircraft that had a 20-foot wingspan and two steam-powered propellers. The model rolled down its inclined launching ramp and executed a brief descending glide, but that was all. It failed to achieve sustained flight. Disheartened at last, Henson gave up the whole business, got married, and in 1848 emigrated to the United States. Stringfellow tested an improved Henson model in 1848, but it was no more successful than its predecessor. Almost as disappointed as Henson had been, Stringfellow took a long vacation from aeronautic research; he would not be heard from again for 20 years.

But the contribution of the two men was more significant than their failures suggest. Henson's design was logically conceived, if only on paper, and his aerial carriage was a plausible expression of what an airplane should be. The showy publicity brought ridicule to the Aerial Transit Company, but it also called worldwide attention to the pursuit of mechanical flight and fixed the vision of an elegant flying machine upon the public mind. Though the tests with the models were unsatisfactory, they were nonetheless a serious attempt to fly a propeller-driven, engine-powered airplane. And the concept of the Aerial Steam Carriage was a lasting stimulus to other inquiring minds.

Even George Cayley, his enthusiasm for aviation undampened by his advancing age, was influenced by the machine. Following up on his own advice to Henson, Cayley made a major departure from his earlier work and began experimenting with a three-winged glider, which he optimistically dubbed a "flyer." As Cayley described it in his notebooks, the craft consisted of a boat-shaped wheeled car with a pilot-operated elevator and rudder; three tiers of wings were affixed atop the car at a dihedral—or shallow V-shaped—angle.

By the spring of 1849 this triplane glider had been put through some brief tests, one of them similar to the flight of a kite. "A boy of about 10 years of age," Cayley wrote later, "was floated off the ground for several yards on descending a hill, and also for about the same space by some persons pulling the apparatus against a very slight breeze by a rope." Cayley did not name his young test pilot, but a friend who learned of the flights wrote of the boy: "Poor fellow! I dare say he feared the fate of some of our early aeronauts."

Then came the 1853 ride of the reluctant coachman, who, on board a glider Cayley called the "new flyer," sailed across the valley near Brompton Hall in true unpowered flight. It is reasonably certain that the vehicle used was an improved version of the boy-carrying glider.

Sarah Cayley, by then totally insane, died one year after the coachman's adventure, and Sir George, his thoughts still on multiwinged gliders and lightweight engines, threw himself into his work. But his strength was failing, and he died on December 15, 1857, twelve days before his 84th birthday, leaving behind an unappreciated legacy of accomplishment. His only surviving son succeeded to the family estates and had the remains of one of Cayley's historic flying machines dragged from its place in the Low Garden to a dilapidated barn, where it reputedly served as a chicken roost.

Cayley's influence far outlasted the fragile fabric and framework of his flying machines and he was later hailed as the towering figure of early aeronautics. The patriotic baronet would hardly have been pleased, however, to know that for a number of years after his death the foremost aviation pioneers would be found not in his own England, but in France, where Cayley's works had first been published in 1853.

Jean-Marie Le Bris, a zesty French sea captain whose active interest in aviation spanned the years between 1856 and 1868, was a man not given to understatement. While voyaging around Cape Horn and the Cape of Good Hope in his younger days, he had frequently observed the graceful wheelings of albatrosses, and once he killed one of the huge birds in order to study it more closely. "I took the wing of the albatross and exposed it to the breeze," he recalled later, "and lo! in spite of me it drew forward into the wind; notwithstanding my resistance it tended to rise. Thus I had discovered the secret of the bird! I comprehended the whole mystery of flight."

Abandoning long sea voyages for short runs along the coast of France, the enthusiastic Le Bris devoted his increased shore time to the construction of a full-sized glider inspired by the albatross. The body of the craft, built to support a pilot, was shaped like a canoe; the narrow, arching wings, each 23 feet long and adjustable by pulleys and cords, provided a lifting surface of 215 square feet. In 1857 Le Bris tested his device by having it pulled down an incline on a horse-drawn cart, and then releasing it against a brisk wind. He succeeded in making a short glide on his first try, but a crash on the second attempt left him with a shattered glider and a broken leg.

By 1868 Le Bris had developed a larger version of his glider, which made several successful test flights, unmanned, before it was smashed to pieces in a crash. Le Bris did not try again.

During the same period in which Le Bris was at work, two other French flight enthusiasts were proceeding along different and somewhat more productive lines. Like Le Bris, they looked to the birds for inspiration; unlike the impulsive sea captain, they made a systematic study of bird flight. Independently, each of them concluded that the action of wind on wings was an important key to the mystery of human flight, and their published observations would have considerable impact on the generation of experimenters to come.

In this promotional illustration, printed on a handkerchief, th

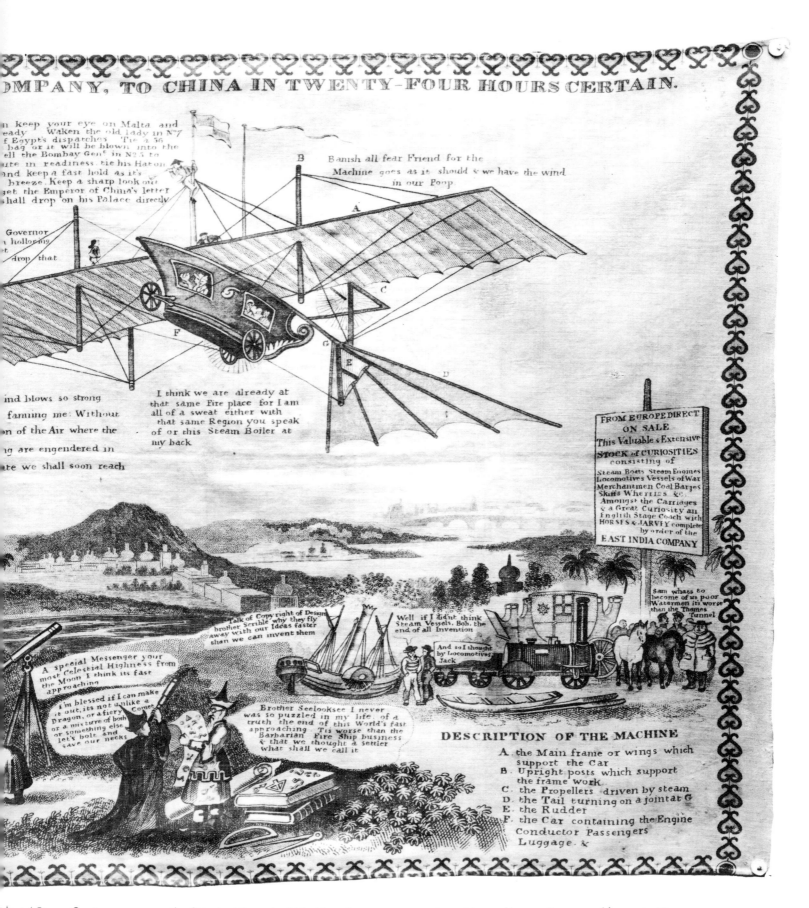

Aerial Steam Carriage soars over the Orient while such old-fashioned conveyances as steamships and locomotives are sold as curiosities.

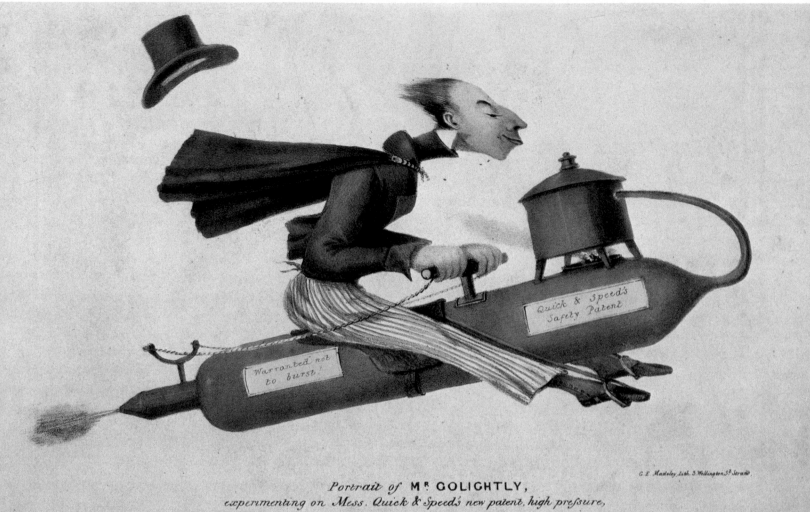

Portrait of MR GOLIGHTLY,
experimenting on Mess. Quick & Speed's new patent, high pressure,
STEAM RIDING ROCKET.

Pub. by C. Tilt, Fleet St

C.E. Madeley, Lith 3 Wellington St Strand

The prophetically streamlined steam rocket in this 1830s engraving is a symbol for the real object of the artist's satire: a newly introduced steam railway locomotive named The Rocket. Steam-powered flight seemed less farfetched a few years later, however, when William Samuel Henson patented his Aerial Steam Carriage.

Count Ferdinand d'Esterno, whose thought-provoking pamphlet, "Du Vol des Oiseaux," was published in 1864, broke new ground with his contention that the wind itself could be a motive power for aircraft, and that a man in a properly designed aerial vehicle could "handle an apparatus carrying 10 tons, just as well as one carrying only his own weight." Louis Mouillard, who had spent a number of years observing the great soaring birds of North Africa, came to a similar conclusion. His book, *The Empire of the Air,* appearing in 1881, advised that man could, "with a rigid surface and properly designed apparatus," soar through the air without the aid of artificial power.

A fourth Frenchman working in France at about the same time was a naval officer named Félix Du Temple, who, if he lacked the exuberant self-confidence of Le Bris, was more fully qualified as an experimental engineer. Aided by his brother, Louis, who was also a naval officer, Du Temple designed and built an ingenious model monoplane drawn by a propeller that was powered first by a clockwork mechanism and later by a small steam engine. In 1857 or 1858 the Du Temple model took off under its own steam, sustained itself in the air for a short distance, and glided down to a safe landing. This was a genuine and important first: the first successful—if brief—flight of a powered airplane of any size.

Du Temple next patented and built a man-carrying monoplane. It had a forward-mounted propeller, wings set at a dihedral angle as originally suggested by Cayley, a lightweight steam engine, a tail plane and rudder, and even a retractable undercarriage. In 1874, with a young French sailor at the controls, the monoplane sped down an inclined ramp at Brest and made a ski-jump takeoff into the air. It could not sustain itself in flight—it apparently landed almost immediately— but Du Temple had at least achieved the first powered hop with a piloted airplane.

Despite this considerable accomplishment, Du Temple did not dominate the field of practical aeronautics in the 1870s. That honor went instead to a brilliant and tragic Frenchman named Alphonse Pénaud. Barred by a disabling hip disease from following his father, an admiral, into the Navy, Pénaud instead applied his training as a marine engineer to aeronautical matters; in 1870, when he was only 20, he developed the twisted rubber band as a power source for model airplanes. He used his invention first in a workable helicopter model—spurring toymakers to produce thousands of rubber-driven helicopter toys—and then in his own more sophisticated airplane models.

In 1871 Pénaud built what he called the "planophore," a monoplane 20 inches long with tapered dihedral wings, an adjustable tail assembly with dihedral tips and a rear-mounted pusher propeller. The craft's wing and tail design made it much more stable than earlier airplane models, and when Pénaud demonstrated his planophore before a group of aeronautical enthusiasts in Paris, it flew 131 feet in 11 seconds—the first flight of an inherently stable aircraft.

Pénaud's next major achievement came in 1876, when he patented his design for a full-sized amphibious monoplane; it included such forward-looking features as a glass-domed two-seated cockpit, a single control column to operate the rear elevators and rudder, and a retractable undercarriage with shock absorbers. But Pénaud was too far ahead of his time. Lack of a lightweight engine stymied his progress, and he was unable to raise funds to build his machine or pursue his research. Frustrated, in failing health and stung by jealous criticism of his work, he committed suicide at the age of 30. Later experimenters, including Wilbur and Orville Wright, would rank Pénaud close to Cayley as one of the most significant 19th Century aeronautical thinkers.

By Pénaud's time, growing numbers of scientists and other researchers were approaching aviation as an engineering problem that could be solved by the human mind. In England, where George Cayley's epic studies had been largely ignored during his lifetime, aviation research had become respectable with the founding of the Aeronautical Society of Great Britain in 1866. At the society's first meeting, its dignified and earnest members listened intently to an address by Francis Herbert Wenham, a marine engineer whose interests ranged from microscopes

to internal-combustion engines. Titled "Aerial Locomotion," his report was to become, like Cayley's three-part article of half a century before, an aviation classic.

Wenham had conducted extensive tests with airfoils and airplane models, and now he advised his fellow enthusiasts that a cambered, or curved, wing was more effective for lift than a flat wing and that a wing's front portion, or leading edge, provided most of the lift required for sustained flight. It was obvious, he said, that a long narrow wing would therefore exert more lift than a short stubby one. Wenham further concluded, as Cayley had, that several such wings, one above another, would provide the greatest lifting area with the least strain. And he advised that prospective fliers should master the control of unpowered gliders in the air before attempting to leave the ground in powered craft.

Wenham had little practical success with his own gliders, which he built with five wings. But he advanced aeronautics significantly, not least by building the first wind tunnel for simulating the movement of variously shaped wing models through the air. His apparatus consisted of a long wooden box with a steam-driven fan at one end, and while Wenham himself conceded that his tests were "somewhat crude and incomplete," later and more sophisticated versions of his equipment became essential tools in aviation research.

In time, Wenham's work would prove useful to both Octave Chanute and the Wright brothers in the United States. But it had a more immediate influence on John Stringfellow, the Englishman who had been absent from the aeronautical scene since the failure of the single-winged Aerial Steam Carriage model he had built with William Henson in the 1840s. Galvanized by Wenham's report to the Aeronautical Society and recalling that Cayley, too, had recommended multiple wing surfaces for heavy aircraft, Stringfellow resurrected the old aerial carriage as a handsome triplane.

Stringfellow showed his new model at the world's first exhibition of

Jean-Marie Le Bris (above, right), a sea captain, made a wavering but successful flight in 1857 in a glider he modeled on an albatross; on his next ascent, however, Le Bris crashed and broke a leg. In 1868 he built an almost identical glider that made several unmanned flights. The second of Le Bris's "artificial birds," as they were called, is shown above, at left, mounted on a cart for easy hauling. The photograph is the first ever taken of a heavier-than-air craft.

Tethered hop of a steam-powered model

Until he was middle-aged, Thomas Moy, a British engineer and patent agent, was an enthusiastic part-time balloonist. Then, in 1865 the inquisitive Englishman decided to turn his attention to the unsolved problem of heavier-than-air flight. Ten years later he was ready to test a remarkable—if flimsy—flying machine *(below)* of his own invention.

In June of 1875, Moy took his so-called Aerial Steamer—a pilotless, tandem-wing monoplane with a three-horsepower steam engine—to the Crystal Palace, the great exhibition hall and park in south London. He placed the 120-pound contraption on a circular launching track, tethered it to one of the park's fountains and fired the boiler. The machine skittered and tugged around the rail—"like a dog on a leash," according to one historian—and eventually managed to lift itself six inches into the air. But Moy apparently had reached the limit of his inventive talent; he contributed little to the field of aviation thereafter.

Thomas Moy's Aerial Steamer, which made a tethered hop in 1875, had a 15-foot wingspan and was driven by fanlike propellers.

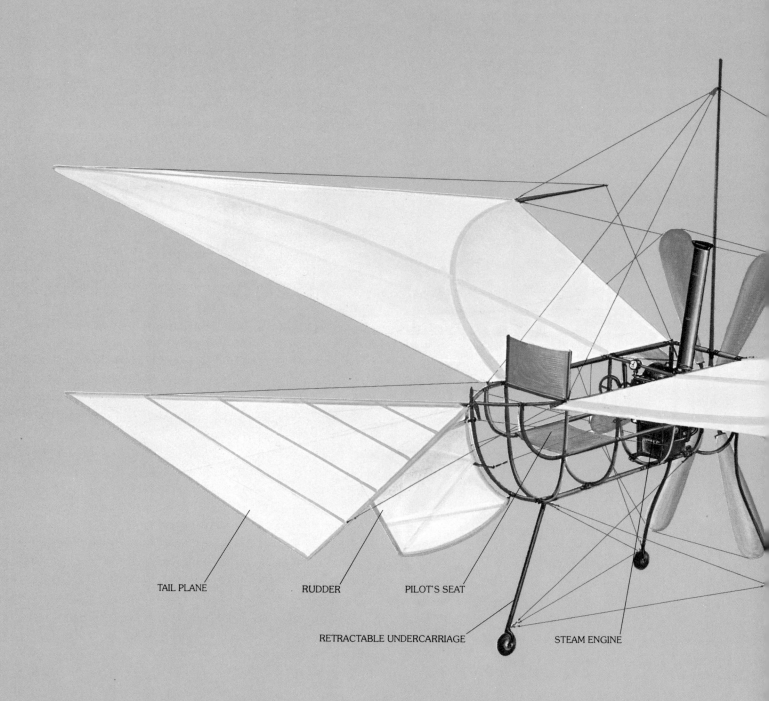

TAIL PLANE

RUDDER

PILOT'S SEAT

RETRACTABLE UNDERCARRIAGE

STEAM ENGINE

The first man-carrying powered aircraft to actually leave the ground was this oddly graceful monoplane created by French naval officer Félix Du Temple. Patented in 1857, it was eventually piloted down an inclined ramp by a French sailor in 1874 but could not sustain itself and landed almost at once. Du Temple's craft was powered by a steam engine that drove a front-mounted propeller; it also featured swept-forward wings, a generous tail plane and rudder, and a retractable undercarriage.

PROPELLER

John Stringfellow's steam-powered triplane
(suspended from the ceiling) was the
center of attention at the first exhibition, in
1868, by Britain's new Aeronautical
Society. Though it never flew, Stringfellow's
triplane influenced subsequent designers,
including the Wright brothers, toward the
use of superposed, or stacked, wings.

flying machines, held in London's Crystal Palace in 1868 and sponsored by the fledgling Aeronautical Society in hopes of presenting aviation as a worthy branch of science. Among the wide assortment of dirigibles, helicopters and flapping ornithopters on display, Stringfellow's steam-powered triplane stood out—even though it was not particularly well designed and failed to perform when tested. Like the old Aerial Steam Carriage, Stringfellow's model captured the public's imagination; for years, illustrations of it continued to appear in publications throughout the world, and laymen and inventors alike were subtly influenced to accept the peculiar configuration of its triplane wings.

Not everyone was captivated by the notion of multiple wings, however; nor did all aeronautical researchers agree with Francis Wenham's conclusion that unpowered gliding would be useful preparation for attempts at engine-driven flight. Indeed, there were some—among them the Frenchman Clément Ader and the American-born Englishman Sir Hiram Maxim—who seemed almost to believe that success could be achieved simply by attaching a sufficiently powerful engine to a pair of wings and roaring into the sky.

Clément Ader, who was to become one of the most controversial figures in aviation history, was born near Toulouse, France, in 1841. A distinguished electrical engineer and inventor who was among the pioneers in the development of the telephone, he also studied the flight of birds and bats, and in 1873 he built a bird-shaped craft with goose-feather wings. Ader did not try to fly this semiglider; instead, he tethered his artificial bird to the ground, nosed it into the wind, and lay prone upon it as stiff breezes raised it to the limit of its anchor ropes.

His curiosity about gliding flight now satisfied, Ader began planning for a powered takeoff. By 1882 he had started the laborious construction of his first aircraft and the exceptionally light steam engine that would be its most remarkable feature.

The Éole, or "god of the winds," was finally ready for testing in October 1890. Resembling nothing so much as a huge bat, it was a monoplane with deeply arched wings that could be moved in four different directions. Its propeller was driven by a 20-horsepower steam engine that brought the craft to a total weight of only 653 pounds, including the operator. In several critical respects the design left much to be desired. The cockpit was located behind the steam boiler, providing almost no forward visibility, and Ader had given little thought to how he might handle the machine if he managed to get it off the ground. The mechanism for controlling the wings was complicated and difficult to operate; there was no elevator, and as far as can be determined, there was no rudder.

Even so, Ader was brimming with confidence on October 9, when he transported the Éole to an estate at Armainvilliers for testing. Only a few assistants witnessed what happened after Ader wheeled his batlike craft to level ground and slipped into the cockpit. By the inventor's own account, he ran up a full head of steam, sped along the ground and rose to a height of about eight inches. Before touching down and rolling to a halt, the *Éole* had traveled through the air for some 165 feet.

If Ader's account is true—and there is little doubt about its essentials—his ungainly machine had thus become the first manned aircraft to take off from level ground under its own power. Yet this feat hardly marked the dawn of human flight. Aerodynamically unsound and too heavy for its small engine, the *Éole,* once airborne, was uncontrollable and incapable of sustained flight.

But the enthusiastic inventor seemed to believe otherwise. Three days after what he confidently referred to as his craft's "first" flight, Ader was almost jubilant about his contribution to aviation progress. "I have resolved the problem," he wrote to a friend, "after much work, fatigue and money." Only the shortness of his test field, he added, had prevented him from flying on for an even greater distance.

Ader soon scaled down his claim, conceding that the first hop had been merely tentative and that more work needed to be done. Meanwhile, in 1892, he found in the French Ministry of War a ready source of funds to support his further research. Commissioned to produce an improved version of the *Éole,* Ader designed and built a twin-engined craft that he called Avion III.

By October 12, 1897, he was ready to put the machine through its paces for military observers who had gathered at a specially prepared circular track on an army post near Versailles. For the first demonstration, Ader merely taxied the Avion III around the track, getting a feel for the vehicle and proving that its two steam-driven propellers were at least capable of moving the machine along the ground. Two days later, toward sunset of a gusty afternoon, he tried to get airborne. But the craft was caught in a strong wind before its wheels could leave the ground. Blown off the track, Ader immediately shut off his hissing engines; the sudden power loss slued the Avion III around and almost overturned it.

The official observers noted in their report that the vehicle was so seriously damaged that further tests would have to be postponed. They also made it absolutely clear that the machine had not raised itself above the ground; the Ministry of War, having already advanced more than 650,000 francs for the development of the Avion III, cut off financial support for the project. A bitterly disappointed Ader complained that the testing arrangements had been unsatisfactory, but he did not quibble with the report's conclusion that he had failed to fly.

Nine years later, however, when the Brazilian-born Alberto Santos-Dumont made a 23-foot powered hop that was hailed in the French press as the first such flight in Europe, Ader began to make inflated claims for himself. He insisted that he not only had made his 165-foot hop aboard the *Éole* in 1890 but that he had gone on to double that distance in a subsequent flight of the same machine. Most curious of all, Ader maintained that the 1897 test of Avion III had been successful and that the military observers had watched him fly nearly 1,000 feet.

This decaying model ornithopter was patented by one R. J. Spalding in 1889. An attached balloon was to help keep it aloft.

Some unlikely designs from Yankee tinkerers

Until practically the end of the 19th Century, most of the major advances in the development of heavier-than-air flying machines were made in Europe. That did not mean that Americans, on their side of the Atlantic, were not trying. For decades, Yankee inventors ranging from college students to the great Thomas Edison attacked the problem of flight with much earnest ingenuity, but scarcely any regard to the achievements—or the failures—of their European contemporaries.

During the latter part of the century the United States Patent Office received patent applications for a dazzling variety of flying machines. Ideas for helicopters were espe-cially popular, as were designs for human-powered ornithopters like the one shown above. Other craft were to be driven by coiled spring, compressed air or electric motor, and swept through the air by propellers, rotors or flappers *(following pages)*.

The Patent Office accepted all of these early designs "without any question as to their operativeness," as one government official put it, "none being thought operative." And, of course, none of them were. Most of the machines never got built and those that did were grounded by the lack of a suitable power plant—if indeed they were at all airworthy to begin with.

W. J. Lewis of New York was reported in 1876 to have flown a 4½-foot model of this winged cabin in a formal test. A clockwork spring drove the model's helicopter rotors and pusher propellers; foot pedals were to power the full-sized version.

This man-powered craft was patented by Theodore Stark of Ottawa, Illinois, in 1893. Its twin airscrews appear effective, but the wing is mounted lengthwise, providing little lift, and there seems to be no provision for steering or landing.

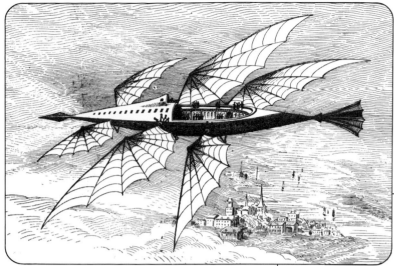

Thomas Edison's contribution to aeronautical design was this six-winged ornithopter that was to be powered by electrical motors and launched from a huge tower. This drawing accompanied an 1880 newspaper interview with Edison.

J. Henry Smith, a student at Princeton, designed this captive helicopter in 1849 as a military observation platform. The rotors above the platform were to be powered by electricity generated by the steam engine below. A parachute above the rotors was insurance in case of power failure.

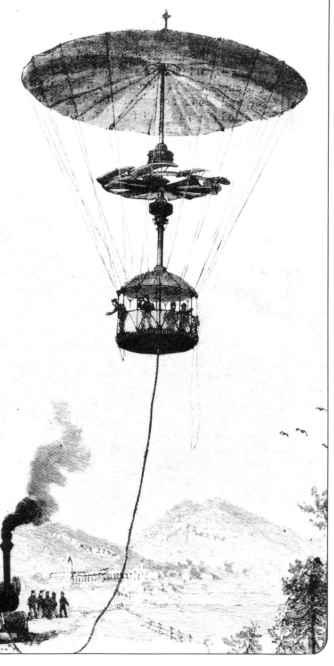

A flying bedframe, designed in 1885 by W. O. Ayres of New Haven, Connecticut, is lifted by six helicopter rotors, four of them powered by compressed air and two driven by the pilot's feet as he simultaneously cranks the pusher propeller, regulates the air supply and controls the rear rudder and forward elevator.

The official report of the abortive 1897 tests had never been published, and Ader managed to persuade the surviving witnesses not to contradict his fanciful story. For years thereafter, Ader's adherents would insist that he had indeed achieved the world's first powered flights, even though his own notebooks and designs testify clearly that he knew nothing of aerodynamics or flight control, and that none of his craft could have flown (except, of course, for *Éole's* brief excursion at the altitude of eight inches).

The enormous and highly publicized winged vehicle that Hiram Maxim built in the early 1890s was equally incapable of sustained and controlled flight. But Maxim's primary concern was merely to "build a flying machine that would lift itself from the ground." By that limited yardstick his experiments were marginally successful, though Maxim himself conceded that problems of aerial steering and control remained to be solved before practical aviation could be achieved.

Maxim had been interested in aeronautics since his boyhood in Maine, where he was born in 1840. When Hiram was 16, his mechanically minded father designed an ingenious two-rotor helicopter, but never attempted to build it—there being no engines light and strong enough to power such a craft. Not long afterward, with less than five years of formal schooling to his credit, young Maxim struck out on his own. Traveling the eastern United States and Canada, he found odd jobs as a carriage painter, cabinetmaker, mechanic or whatever happened along. In his spare time he studied science and engineering— and dreamed up practical jokes. Once he put phosphorus in a friend's hair oil; when the young man went out walking with his girl, his hair glowed in the dark.

At the age of 24, Maxim signed on as an apprentice at his uncle's engineering works in Fitchburg, Massachusetts. While there, he gained impressive skills in draftsmanship, wood turning, brass finishing and coppersmithing; decades later, when he himself employed a large staff of workmen, Maxim still enjoyed showing off his mastery of blacksmithing and glass blowing. "There's nothing that the old man can't do!" his employees would say admiringly.

In the early 1870s Maxim moved to New York, where he became chief engineer for one of the nation's first electric utilities. Toward the end of the decade he invented a machine gun and showed it to the United States War and Navy Departments; both agencies found the gun ingenious but impractical, and turned it down. But when Maxim made a business trip to London in 1881, he found the British War Office considerably more interested in his ideas, and he decided to settle in England. Eventually he became a British subject, though he displayed the Stars and Stripes in his home and considered the United States the only safe country in which to invest his money. In 1884 he perfected the 600-rounds-per-minute Maxim machine gun, a devastating weapon that made him rich and famous. The machine gun proved so valuable to the

French engineer Clément Ader (in a self-portrait above) spent eight years building a curious steam-powered monoplane, the Éole, shown in a fanciful engraving (right).

The Éole never flew in the manner this 1891 magazine cover suggests, but it did lift off —by less than a foot —under its own power.

Hiram Maxim demonstrates the lightness of his 180-hp steam engine.

British in military engagements that the inventor eventually was knighted by Queen Victoria.

Maxim's youthful interest in aviation revived in the late 1880s. He began to study wing forms and propellers—first on a whirling arm and then in a wind tunnel. After proving to his own satisfaction that heavier-than-air flight was possible, he turned his considerable talents to the development of a powerful but lightweight steam engine. At the same time he rented Baldwyns Park, a manorial estate in Kent, where there was ample room to construct work sheds and a track for testing his proposed aircraft.

Writing in the June 1892 issue of *The Cosmopolitan* magazine, Maxim described the kind of craft he had in mind. When building a flying machine, he said, "it is neither necessary nor practical to imitate the bird too closely, because screw propellers have been found to be very efficient" when operated at sufficient speed to produce thrust. "Without doubt," he continued, "the motor is the chief thing to be considered. Scientists have long said, Give us a motor and we will very soon give you a successful flying machine."

Maxim's finished flying machine reflected this preoccupation with powerful engines. It was an enormous biplane equipped with two 180-horsepower steam engines, each driving a pusher propeller nearly 18 feet in diameter. The platform for the engines, boiler and a three-man crew was 40 feet long and eight feet wide; the craft measured about 200 feet from tip to tail and had a 107-foot wingspan. To provide stability, Maxim placed an elevator fore and aft and set the outer wing panels at a

Maxim's four-ton flying machine, powered by the steam engine he devised, rests on its 1,800-foot test track. The inventive Maxim had devoted almost as much thought to the track as to the machine. The track's outer rails allowed the craft to rise slightly, but kept it from lifting off completely and crashing.

Members of the Aeronautical Society and other scientists visiting Hiram Maxim (seated, center) in 1895 are dwarfed by his invention.

dihedral angle. The great craft had a total lifting surface of 4,000 square feet and weighed an incredible 8,000 pounds, including crew.

Maxim built an ingenious two-level track for testing his machine. The lower track, built of heavy steel rails, was the runway, engaged by the four cast-iron wheels of the undercarriage. The upper track, made of three-by-nine-inch Georgia pine, was intended to keep the ponderous biplane from escaping its test track and lofting into uncontrollable flight: If the machine rose more than a few inches from its runway, a second set of smaller wheels would engage the wooden guardrails and hold the vehicle down.

Though dogged by mishaps and breakdowns during test runs toward the end of 1892 and early 1893, the Maxim machine in motion was an awesome sight. Journalist H. J. W. Dam, visiting the "jolly, even boisterous" Maxim in 1893, took a ride on his host's huge biplane. When full steam was up and the propellers were spinning so fast that they seemed to have become whirling disks, Maxim shouted, "Let go!" Then, "A rope was pulled, the machine shot forward like a railway train, and, with the big wheels whirling, the steam hissing, and the waste pipes puffing and gurgling, flew over the eighteen hundred feet of track in much less time than it takes to tell it."

"Flew" was a figure of speech; the machine did not really fly, then or ever. On its final test run, on July 31, 1894, Maxim drove the craft at high boiler pressure along the track. After covering 600 feet and gaining a speed of 42 miles per hour, the machine lifted from its steel runway and rose until the secondary wheels reached the wooden guardrails. Suddenly, one of the rails snapped. The machine was liberated "and floated in the air," Maxim wrote afterward, giving those on board the sensation of being in a boat. But not for long. A chunk of broken guardrail smashed into a propeller, and Maxim immediately shut off the steam. His clumsy and uncontrollable flying machine came to a quick halt and settled to the ground, never to rise again.

Maxim had demonstrated that a powerful engine could lift a heavy winged object from the ground—a proposition that had already been accepted by the aeronautical experts of his time. He was too busy with his other affairs to continue his aviation experiments, though he would later make absurd claims that he had been the first to think out all the elements incorporated in the earliest successful airplane.

Even though he contributed little to aeronautical progress, Maxim's reputation and his widely reported experiments helped convince the public that the age of heavier-than-air flight was nearly at hand. And Maxim was also a good prophet. Even "under the most unfavorable circumstances," he told a journalist in 1893, "aerial navigation will be an accomplished fact inside of ten years."

Before that could happen, however, the initiative in aeronautical research would have to be seized by men whose approach to the problem of practical flight was considerably different from the powerful-engine school of Clément Ader and Hiram Maxim.

3
Learning to ride the wind

One can get a proper insight into the practice of flying only by actual flying experiments," wrote Otto Lilienthal in 1896. "The manner in which we have to meet the irregularities of the wind, when soaring in the air, can only be learned by being in the air itself."

Lilienthal was a dominant figure in aeronautics during the decade before the development of powered airplanes. Illustrated reports of the German glider enthusiast's successful soarings were published throughout the world, earning him a far-flung reputation as "the flying man." Yet for all his impact on aeronautical progress, Lilienthal's zestful commitment to get on "intimate terms with the wind" was not widely copied by his fellow European researchers. The Frenchman Clément Ader and the influential Hiram Maxim of England, loudly insisting that mighty engines were the key to human flight, denigrated the need for gliding as a prelude to powered flight. Indeed, Maxim spoke of Lilienthal as a mere parachutist, likening him to a flying squirrel. Lilienthal replied in kind, observing that Maxim's one accomplishment with his hulking steam plane was to show others how not to fly.

In fact, each could have learned from the other, but a climate of rivalry and mutual suspicion barred an exchange of ideas that might have hastened the coming of powered flight. The American editor James Means wrote in his influential *Aeronautical Annual* for 1895: "If any two men should be friends rather than foes, these are the two. Each has certain ideas and qualifications which the other lacks, and it is the greatest of pities that they cannot clasp hands over the watery channel."

In the United States too a growing community of aviation enthusiasts sought their common goal along the different paths charted by Maxim and Lilienthal. But American researchers were generally more willing than their European counterparts to share ideas and heed the findings of those whose approaches differed from their own. The publications of Means in Boston, and Octave Chanute in Chicago, became forums for divergent views as they spread the word about the intriguing work of European pioneers like Maxim and Germany's "flying man."

Otto Lilienthal was born in 1848 in the Pomeranian village of Anklam, where he and his younger brother, Gustav, were fascinated by the soaring flight of the storks that nested in the region. The brothers were still in their teens when they conducted their first crude aeronautical experiment by building a frail contraption of thin birch veneer; it had

Two barefoot school children stare at Otto Lilienthal drifting to earth in a biplane glider near Berlin in 1895. Lilienthal tested two biplanes during that year, flying them in winds of more than 24 mph. The German engineer's persistent, systematic and intelligent approach to the problem of flight led Wilbur Wright to call him "the greatest of the precursors."

The Lilienthal brothers—Otto stands next to Gustav in this 1863 photograph—held their earliest experiments at night, "to escape the jibes of our school-mates."

a pair of six-and-a-half-foot strap-on wings with which they intended to dash down a hillside and, by flapping their arms, take off storklike into the air. An uncle predicted disaster for the venture, but their widowed mother urged them on.

Their wings failed to lift the young Lilienthals, but they were undaunted and built two more winged vehicles. These failed, too, but Otto kept his faith in human flight. He studied at technical academies in Potsdam and Berlin. Although his aeronautical pursuits were interrupted by service in the Franco-Prussian War of 1870-1871, his infantry comrades recalled that he could speak of little except his dream of building a flying machine. "Now," he said to Gustav when he returned with his regiment to Berlin, "we shall finish it." But Gustav had become increasingly busy with a budding career as an architect, and Otto was left to follow his aeronautical interests alone.

Once back in civilian life, Otto concentrated on a career in engineer-

Otto Lilienthal descends a hillside at Derwitz in 1891 in his first successful glider. Called simply No. 3, it had a wing area of 86 square feet and weighed 40 pounds.

ing and in 1880 he opened his own factory in Berlin, manufacturing such items as small steam engines and marine foghorns. Later, he would build his Flug-Apparat, or flying machine, there. But before he tried again to fly, he studied the principles of flight.

Writing of this go-slow approach, Lilienthal noted that other men had first built their full-blown flying machines, and then sought to fly them. But he, said Lilienthal, had determined "that our physical and technical knowledge and our practical experience were by far insufficient to overcome a mechanical task of such magnitude without more preliminaries." One such preliminary, rooted in his youthful observation of birds, was the conclusion that "the arched or vaulted wing includes the secret of the art of flight."

Sir George Cayley had recognized the lifting value of cambered surfaces almost 100 years before, but he had envisaged a curvature that was caused and maintained by upward air pressure on a wing made of fabric. Lilienthal, on the other hand, believed that a rigidly cambered wing would be required, and in the workshop of his suburban Berlin home he built test equipment—some of it reminiscent of Cayley's whirling-arm device—to measure the amount of lift that would be produced by various wing shapes. Lilienthal's experiments clearly demonstrated the superior lifting quality of the curved wing, and in 1889 he published his findings in a book that almost at once became a classic of aeronautical literature, *Birdflight as the Basis of Aviation.* In it he spelled out in detail his studies of wing structure and the dynamics of bird flight, and he included a description of how birds propel themselves by the twisting, or airscrew, action of their outer primary feathers. Most interesting of all to other experimenters were the tables that showed Lilienthal's painstaking calculations of the lift provided by wings with various degrees of camber.

Lilienthal's firm belief in gliding as a preliminary to mastering powered flight led him in 1891 to begin experimenting with a series of unpowered craft, their lightweight willow frameworks covered with tightly stretched fabric. Most were fixed-wing monoplanes, though he would later experiment with biplane designs. In a report published in the United States by the Smithsonian Institution in 1893, he described a cautious start that echoed Bishop John Wilkins' centuries-old advice, to approach flying one step at a time. "The first attempts," Lilienthal wrote, "were made from a grass plot in my own garden upon which, at a height of one meter from the ground, I had erected a springboard, from which the leap with my sailing apparatus gave me an oblique descent through the air. After several hundred of these leaps I gradually increased the height of my board to 2½ meters, and from that

Leaping from a tower that also stored his gliders, Lilienthal soars over the heads of spectators at Maihöhe in 1893. The tower roof was some 30 feet above the base of the hill and Lilienthal wrote that from this height, "after sufficient practice," he could glide more than 50 yards.

elevation I could safely and without danger cross the entire grass plot.''

After exhausting the limited range of his own backyard, Lilienthal tried several other test locations that offered more flying room. In 1894 he constructed an artificial hill not far from his home and topped it with a wooden, earth-covered hangar for storing his machines. Running downhill from the summit and leaping into the face of the wind, he repeatedly achieved glides of 150 feet and more, many of them witnessed by such distinguished visitors as the American professor Samuel Langley, Secretary of the Smithsonian Institution. Langley, who was experimenting with steam-powered aircraft models at the time, was not particularly impressed with the appearance of Lilienthal's gliders. "The aspect of the whole was heavy and clumsy," he wrote to an associate, although he conceded that the German's ungainly craft performed handsomely in the air.

Less concerned with appearances than with obtaining flight practice, Lilienthal sought yet another site that would offer not only height for launching but strong and constant winds. He found such a place in the Rhinower Hills about six miles northwest of Berlin, and beginning in 1894 he went there every Sunday to try out his flying machines. Launching himself from halfway up 164-foot hills, he achieved spectacular glides of up to 1,150 feet. At a time when powered "aircraft" were still lumbering along on the ground, such performances were cheering evidence that man could fly through the air—though without an engine—in a heavier-than-air vehicle.

More than anyone before him, Lilienthal came to know and trust the ocean of the air. "No one," he would say, "can realize how *substantial* the air is, until he feels its supporting power beneath him. It inspires

In 1893 Lilienthal took out an American patent on glider No. 6 (below), whose wings folded up for easier transportation and storage. In the photograph at bottom, taken the following year, he lands in No. 6 at the base of a hill he had built near Berlin. From its top he could take off in any direction, depending on the prevailing wind.

confidence at once." But in an article for the Smithsonian Institution's *Annual Report* for 1893, he cautioned that the wind was "a treacherous fellow"; the man who would fly must proceed cautiously, achieving stability through the design of his flying machine and by his flight-control system. A flying machine's balance, Lilienthal explained, is constantly shifting, and stable flight can be maintained only "by a constant and arbitrary correction of the position of the center of gravity."

Lilienthal balanced his own craft by throwing his weight around in a series of acrobatic body movements that kept the glider flying on an even keel. A typical flight was described by R. W. Wood, a reporter for the *Boston Evening Transcript*, who accompanied Lilienthal to the grassy hills of Rhinower one Sunday afternoon in 1896. Lilienthal was dressed in his usual flying costume of flannel shirt, heavy shoes, snug-fitting cap, and knickerbockers with the knees thickly padded in case of a rough landing. With an assistant's help he carried the machine to the top of a hill and took his place in a rectangular frame beneath and between the wings. Lifting the craft from the ground, he grasped a crossbar and rested his forearms on a pair of small cushions that were attached to the main frame.

The reporter, armed with a camera, wrote later that he took up a position downhill and waited for Lilienthal, who "faced the wind and stood like an athlete waiting for the starting pistol. Presently the breeze freshened; he took three rapid steps forward and was instantly lifted from the ground, sailing off nearly horizontally from the summit. He went over my head at a terrific pace, at an elevation of about 50 feet, the wind playing wild tunes on the tense cordage of the machine, and was past me before I had time to train the camera on him."

Then, all at once: "The apparatus tipped sideways as if a sudden gust had got under the left wing. For a moment I could see the top of the aeroplane, and then, with a powerful throw of his legs he brought the machine once more on an even keel, and sailed away below me across the fields at the bottom, kicking at the tops of the haycocks as he passed over them. When within a foot of the ground he threw his legs forward, and notwithstanding its great velocity the machine stopped instantly, its front turning up, allowing the wind to strike under the wings, and he dropped lightly to the earth."

For those occasions when his descent was not quite so gentle, Lilienthal had incorporated a shock-absorbing device into a glider he built in 1894. Called the *prellbügel,* or rebound bow, it was a flexible willow hoop fitted in front of the pilot's position to act as a resilient bumper guard upon landing. At least once it saved Lilienthal's life.

"During a gliding flight taken from a great height," Lilienthal wrote of the near-fatal occasion, "the center of gravity lay too much to the back; at the same time I was unable—owing to fatigue—to draw the upper part of my body again toward the front." Overloaded in the rear, the machine shot skyward, stalled and then nose-dived toward the earth from a height of more than 60 feet. The *prellbügel* splintered as it buried

Though it claimed to be a "scrupulously exact" reproduction of a photograph of an accident in which Otto Lilienthal "suffered serious injuries," this 1894 cover from Le Petit Parisien is in fact an imaginative fraud. Lilienthal did fall, but he was nowhere near a convenient roof to grab onto, no photographers were present, and all that he suffered was a sprained wrist and a slight cut on the head.

Le Petit Parisien

SUPPLÉMENT LITTÉRAIRE ILLUSTRÉ

TOUS LES JOURS
e Petit Parisien
5 CENTIMES

DIRECTION : 18, rue d'Enghien, PARIS

TOUS LES JEUDIS
SUPPLÉMENT LITTÉRAIRE
5 CENTIMES

L'HOMME-VOLANT

itself in the ground, but it absorbed the shock of impact and Lilienthal escaped with minor injuries. His crash landing did not dampen his enthusiasm for future glides (nor did it persuade him to install the *prellbügel* on all his gliders).

For all his practical experience, Lilienthal had one blind spot. He believed unswervingly that flapping wings were the answer to aerial locomotion. First in 1893 and again in 1895 he built powered devices with ornithopter features. Each machine was fitted with a lightweight carbonic acid gas engine, producing about 2 horsepower, that was supposed to make the wing tips flap and thus drive the craft ahead. The first model was so ineffective that he did not even attempt to fly it; the second malfunctioned during its trial runs and did not achieve horizontal flight.

Lilienthal was never able to give these curiously old-fashioned machines another test. On August 9, 1896, he took off from a hill in the Rhinower range in one of his standard monoplane gliders. A sudden sharp gust tossed his machine upward at an acute angle. Lilienthal immediately threw his weight forward and tried to bring the nose down. But the craft stalled, its left wing dipped sharply and the machine plunged to the ground. This time there was no *prellbügel* to cushion the impact. Otto Lilienthal—who had frequently said that many sacrifices would have to be made on the road to manned flight—died the next day of a broken spine.

Otto Lilienthal's flight research had probably taken him about as far as he could go. His concept of wing-flapping propulsion was a blind alley, as was his approach to the problems of stability and control. He crashed because his machine was unstable, and controllable only by human strength and agility. These qualities were not adequate for successful sustained flight, nor could they readily be incorporated in a practical flying machine.

Despite his limitations, Lilienthal's influence on aviation was incalculable. He was the quintessential airman, the personification of man in flight. His writings were translated and read throughout the world. Newspaper reporters and magazine writers who had made tentative test flights with his gliders wrote glowing accounts of the wonderful sensation of soaring. Widely distributed photographs of the German flying master in action showed a fascinated public that man could indeed sustain himself in the air on artificial wings. Other aviation enthusiasts studied his work, sought his advice and copied his machines.

Among those inspired by Lilienthal's example was the Scotsman Percy Sinclair Pilcher, who was an assistant lecturer in naval architecture and marine engineering at the University of Glasgow when he built his first glider, called the *Bat*, in 1895. The *Bat* was much like the standard Lilienthal monoplane hang glider pictured in the newspapers except that it lacked a horizontal stabilizer. With commendable prudence, Pilcher decided to visit Lilienthal and practice in proven machines before flying his own craft.

After Otto Lilienthal's fatal crash in 1896 this bronze medal was struck in his memory. One side is inscribed in German: "The first human flight of the greatest teacher."

Lilienthal generously allowed Pilcher to gain gliding experience with him and made a number of suggestions for improving the *Bat.* Pilcher followed the advice and went on to build other gliders—the *Beetle,* the *Gull* and the *Hawk*—of increasingly effective design. The *Hawk,* completed in 1896, the year of Lilienthal's death, was a particularly successful hang glider, with cambered wings, a tail unit that hinged upward and a wheeled undercarriage fitted with springs. Using a rope-and-pulley system to launch his craft, Pilcher was able to glide for distances of up to 750 feet.

Pilcher next intended to build a powered version of the *Hawk,* its four-foot propeller driven by a small gasoline engine of about 4 horsepower. Pilcher planned to take off in this machine by running down a hill; once the craft was in the air the propeller would be started, and the machine would fly on—or so he hoped—at about 30 miles per hour.

Pilcher had completed his engine by 1899, but experiments with a new triplane glider and attempts to form a company to promote his machines kept him from completing and testing his powered craft. Then on September 30 he staged a gliding demonstration for a group of English aeronautical enthusiasts who had assembled on the estate of Lord Braye at Stanford Hall in Leicestershire.

The day was dank and dismal, and for some reason Pilcher's gliders had been left outdoors for several hours. All were sodden and heavy by flight time, but Pilcher decided to go on with the show. His first launch in the well-tested *Hawk* ended in a premature but gentle landing. On the second try, the waterlogged craft soared to an altitude of about 30 feet—then a soggy bamboo rod in the tail assembly gave way with a snap. The whole tail unit collapsed and the *Hawk* plummeted to the ground. The 33-year-old Percy Pilcher died two days later without regaining consciousness.

Two years before his fatal crash, Pilcher had written prophetically that his gliders were mere practice vehicles, to be employed only until the advent of engines that could drive an aircraft forward. "Then," he said, "a person who is used to sailing down a hill with a simple soaring machine will be able to fly with comparative safety." But that great leap from soaring to powered flight was not destined to be made in Europe. Following the deaths of the inspirational Lilienthal and the determined Pilcher, the scattered community of European aviation enthusiasts made little headway. Indeed, the torch of aeronautical progress was already passing to the United States, which had its own source of inspiration—and information—in the somewhat unlikely person of a sexagenarian bridge builder named Octave Chanute.

Born in Paris in 1832, Chanute emigrated to America with his parents when he was six. In 1849, after completing his formal education at a private school in New York City and deciding on a career in civil engineering, he traveled to the nearby village of Sing Sing to apply for a construction job with the Hudson River Railroad. Taken on as an un-

A daredevil show of high-gliding

As early as 1884, when he was 26, John J. Montgomery of California made the first of several flights in a camber-winged glider with a rear stabilizer; though the importance of his contributions is a matter of dispute, his advocates consider him the "father of basic flying."

Still working with gliders 20 years later, Montgomery in 1905 demonstrated a tandem-winged craft that was lifted to 4,000 feet by a hot-air balloon. The glider's pilot, daredevil parachutist Dan Maloney, then cut the towline. The glider sailed through several turns, then landed gently at a preselected spot.

That was the apogee of Montgomery's efforts. A second demonstration (*opposite*) was marred by mishaps; 10 weeks later Maloney was killed when the glider crashed, and in 1911 Montgomery lost his life in the same way.

Designer J. J. Montgomery, wearing a bowler hat, stands with pilot Dan Maloney beside the glider Santa Clara in April 1905. Maloney claimed to be able to control the direction of the glider by moving wires that were attached to the four wings.

"Winged Man Sweeps Skyward"

MOST DARING FEAT
EVER ACCOMPLISHED BY MAN

ONLY CHANCE TO WITNESS THIS MARVELOUS SCIENTIFIC WONDER

THE MONTGOMERY AEROPLANE

TAKING LESSONS FROM THE BIRDS

ADMISSION 25¢. CHILD'N 10¢.

A poster touts a second Montgomery exhibition, held in May 1905 at a race track in San Jose, California (right). The balloon lifted off, but the glider accidentally was released too soon and the angry crowd did not think it got its quarter's worth.

paid worker until he proved his aptitude for hard work, he was soon making the respectable sum of $1.12½ a day. It was the start of a brilliant career that ultimately brought him recognition as one of the nation's most gifted civil engineers. Chanute branched out, from railroading to bridge building to architecture to wood preservation. Among the more famous of his design and construction projects were the vast Union Stock Yards in Chicago and the bridge across the Missouri River at Kansas City; after a dazzling series of such engineering successes, he settled down in Chicago with his wife and family in 1890 and established his own engineering firm.

Chanute was always rather vague about how or why he first became interested in aeronautics. Unlike Cayley and Lilienthal, he could claim no boyhood fascination with birds, but he seems to have been intrigued as an adult by the technical problems of human flight. Reading an article by the French modelmaker Alphonse Pénaud in the 1876 *Annual Report* of the Aeronautical Society of Great Britain, Chanute began to consider the lifting properties of the wind—his thinking conditioned by his experience as an engineer.

For many years, he recalled later, he had been aware "that there were a number of observed wind phenomena, such as the lifting of roofs, the blowing off of bridges, and the tipping over of locomotives, which the known velocity and pressure of the wind at the time was insufficient to account for." It was only a short step from that awareness to a study of the wind's influence on heavy airborne objects.

Despite his many other interests, Chanute found time to pursue his investigations into aerodynamics, collecting material on heavier-than-air flight from the days of ancient wing flappers to the latest scientific gliding experiments. Chanute's growing knowledge of aeronautical history and development prompted his friend Mathias Nace Forney, editor of the *Railroad and Engineering Journal,* to ask him to write a series of articles on the development of the flying machine. Chanute plunged enthusiastically into the task, sifting old writings and gathering yet more information from leading aeronautical experimenters, many of whom he met when he presented well-received papers at two scientific conferences—in Paris and Toronto—in 1889. He carried on a brisk correspondence with researchers all over the world, and was soon regarded as a source of inspiration and a one-man clearinghouse for news of the latest developments in aviation. Sometimes he offered more than encouragement and information, supplying his correspondents with money to continue their work.

The first of Chanute's articles appeared in October 1891, and they continued for 27 issues. In 1894 the articles were reprinted in book form, with additional material, under the title *Progress in Flying Machines.* Along with Otto Lilienthal's work on bird flight, the book became a bible of aviation, offering a comprehensive survey of the attempts that had been made, a critique of the results and a guide to further research and development.

While an assistant stands by to steady the wing, Scottish aviation pioneer Percy Pilcher (right) prepares to take to the air in his most successful glider, the Hawk, in 1898. The following year, the Hawk's tail collapsed in flight and Pilcher was killed.

Chanute's work had rapidly expanded his circle of American aeronautical acquaintances, and it was soon clear that the United States had a rich supply of obscure but budding aviation researchers. One correspondent, John J. Montgomery of California, had made a successful glider flight as early as the mid-1880s. Israel Lancaster, born to an Illinois farm family, had gained a considerable reputation as an ornithologist and had flown a series of bird models—which he sometimes called "soaring effigies"—to demonstrate his theories of flight. A young man from Tennessee named Edward C. Huffaker had begun making small gliding models in 1892.

Under Chanute's tireless influence, these and other men were brought together in a loose family of aviation enthusiasts who shared ideas and sometimes worked together. And toward the end of 1894, Chanute took his own first leap from theory to practice and made preparations to test a variety of gliders.

His correspondence had turned up three fellow enthusiasts who were eager to work for him. One was Augustus M. Herring, a New Yorker who had built several unsuccessful gliders before progressing to more effective Lilienthal-type designs in which he had made glides of up to 150 feet. For a time, Herring collaborated with Chanute by mail, but in late 1895 he moved to Chicago and started the construction of a Lilienthal-type glider at Chanute's expense. William Avery, a Chicago carpenter and electrician, was hired at the same time to build a Chanute-designed multiwing glider under Herring's supervision. The fourth member of the team was William Paul Butusov, a Russian immigrant whose early years had been spent at sea and who claimed to have built a successful glider modeled after Jean-Marie Le Bris's artificial birds. Chanute offered to finance a new version of Butusov's birdlike craft for testing along with the Herring and Avery machines.

The first trials were scheduled for the spring of 1896. Butusov's *Albatross* was not ready in time, but Chanute proceeded with his other flight-test plans. He had chosen a site among the dunes on the south shore of Lake Michigan, about 30 miles east of Chicago, where winds had blown the soft yellow sand from the beach into hills rising from 70 to 300 feet above the lake. Chanute and his small band of experimenters arrived on June 22 and pitched camp on the windblown shore. According to Chanute's diary, Herring immediately assembled the "Lilienthal machine" and proceeded to take several jumps with it. But Chanute noted that the glider was "cranky," and Herring's longest glide for the first day was no more than about 70 feet.

As if that beginning were not disheartening enough, further distraction was provided by the arrival of a number of onlookers. One of the unwelcome visitors telegraphed to Chicago that flying experiments were being made, and a reporter from the *Chicago Tribune* arrived at the scene the next day. From then on the test site was seldom free from curious sightseers. Tests had barely started before newspapermen began filing stories about the strange doings on the dunes, and readers all across the nation eagerly followed the exploits of the airborne Chicagoans.

For the first week, the four men concentrated on testing Herring's Lilienthal-type glider, which did not fare well in the ever-changing wind. Gusts whipped it in all directions while the operator tried to steady it for the running takeoff. "Once under way the same action continued," Chanute reported in the 1897 *Aeronautical Annual,* "and the operator was compelled to shift his weight constantly, like a tight-rope dancer without a pole, in order to bring the center of gravity directly under the center of pressure and to avoid being upset."

The Lilienthal-type apparatus was taken up for about 100 glides, in winds ranging from 12 to 17 miles per hour. The longest glide was 116 feet. Chanute himself did not venture into the air, observing that he "was no longer young and active enough to perform such acrobatic exercises without breaking the apparatus." Even in the more adroit hands of the three younger men, the Lilienthal machine was damaged a number of times; after several mendings, it flipped over on a landing and was shattered beyond repair. "Glad to be rid of it," wrote Chanute

A fruitful summer of aerial tests

During June and August of 1896, aviation authority Octave Chanute camped on the southern shore of Lake Michigan experimenting with man-carrying gliders. He was accompanied by three younger protégés—William Avery, Augustus Herring and William Butusov—who made scores of flights in gliders of their own and Chanute's design.

Scholarly research and writing about aeronautics had already earned Chanute a worldwide reputation. But he said later that he learned more about flight in two weeks of practical experimentation than he had in years of theoretical study.

OCTAVE CHANUTE

Chanute, too old to fly himself, poses in the first version of the Katydid while Avery (left) and Herring help steady the craft.

Octave Chanute, third from left, and his crew endure the presence of two newspapermen (far right) at their August camp. The reporters had discovered Chanute's whereabouts when he sent for a tent to replace one ripped to shreds by a storm his first night out.

The Chanute-Herring biplane glider lifts off to a good start on a test flight in August 1896. Weighing 23 pounds and having a total wing area of 135 square feet, the glider could carry a 155-pound pilot.

William Butusov's bat-winged Albatross is poised for takeoff from its launching ramp. Its performance disappointed Chanute.

in his diary entry of June 29—less than two weeks before Lilienthal died aboard a similar craft.

After Herring's glider had demonstrated its lack of stability and control, the four men turned to the apparatus built by William Avery to Chanute's specifications. Its multiwing design was based on Chanute's firm belief that a successful flying machine must be inherently stable, maintaining equilibrium automatically at all angles and under all wind conditions without the intervention of the pilot. As Chanute wrote later, the glider "was based upon just the reverse of the principles involved in the Lilienthal apparatus. Instead of the man moving about, to bring the center of gravity under the center of pressure, it was intended that the wings should move automatically so as to bring the movable center of pressure back over the center of gravity, which latter would remain fixed. That is to say, that the wings should move instead of the man."

Chanute's glider had no fewer than 12 wings, each six feet long by three feet wide, arranged one above another. They were attached to the central frame by pivots that permitted them to swing forward or backward to balance the craft whenever a change in the wind occurred. And the frame was designed so the wings could be grouped in various combinations at the front or rear, permitting the experimenters to determine the best arrangement for maximum lift as well as equilibrium.

Chanute's associates had not been impressed by the multiplane when they tested it during the first week at the dunes. "All are afraid because of its novelty," Chanute observed in his diary. But as various changes were made in the wing groupings—five pairs in front and one at the tail seemed to work best—the operators found it easier and easier to handle. They even grew fond of it, naming it the Katydid because of its insect-like appearance. At the five to one configuration, the machine proved to be "steady, safe, and manageable in winds up to 20 miles an hour." Herring and Avery made many short glides with it, the longest being an 82-foot hop by Herring.

The glides had not covered exceptional distances, but Chanute was pleased with his experiments. He had learned much about the inconstancy of the wind and the principles governing the equilibrium of a man-carrying machine. On the afternoon of July 4 the group packed up and returned to Chicago to see their families and build more gliders.

Avery's Chicago workshop hummed with activity for the next several weeks as three machines took shape: Butusov's *Albatross,* a rebuilt Katydid and a new craft jointly designed by Chanute and Herring. This new machine was to have fixed wings, unlike the Katydid's multiple movable surfaces, and a combined horizontal and vertical rudder. The three wings were braced, one above another, with a type of truss that Chanute had used many times in building bridges.

On August 21 the party went back to the sand hills for a second round of tests. This time, hoping to avoid the prying eyes of unwanted spectators, they pitched camp five miles farther down the beach, "where the hills were higher, the solitude greater, and the path more obscure to the railroad." Curiosity seekers showed up all the same, but more than a few would-be visitors got lost while picking their way through woods and swamps to the launching site.

After a spell of stormy weather, the trials got under way on August 29. Butusov's *Albatross,* a heavy craft that required a special launching ramp for takeoff, achieved no more than a few short, steep glides. The improved Katydid did considerably better, more than doubling its previous distance record. But it was the bridge-trussed Chanute-Herring glider that surpassed all expectations and brought a sustained sense of excitement to the camp.

This craft had been built as a triplane, but Herring decided that the lowest wing was unnecessary and removed it. Over the course of 14 days the new biplane made scores of glides in wind speeds that ranged from 10 miles per hour to a strong 31. Both Avery and Herring made several unusually good flights, the best of which were comparable to those of Lilienthal: 256 feet in 10.2 seconds for Avery, and 359 feet in 14 seconds for Herring. Chanute, gratified by the craft's gradual angle of descent as well as by its maneuverability, wrote that the biplane was "steady, easy to handle before starting, and under good control when under way—a motion of the operator's body of not over two inches proving as effective as a motion of five or more inches in the Lilienthal machine."

By the time the tests ended on September 26, the experimenters had become so confident of both the biplane and the multiplane that they offered free rides to visitors bold enough to try. The offer was taken up by a number of neophytes, some of whom sailed as far as 150 feet. "All agreed," wrote Chanute, "that the sensation of coasting on the air was delightful." At a time when heavier-than-air aviation was virtually moribund in Europe, the rankest amateurs were joy riding through the air on the shores of Lake Michigan.

The experiments convinced Chanute that it was possible to develop an inherently stable craft that could maintain aerial balance without the gyrations of an acrobatic pilot. In his judgment, however, considerably more research with gliders would be required before it would be prudent to add an engine to a flying machine.

Herring disagreed, and even before the season's tests were over he broke from the Chanute group to work on a powered machine inspired by the Chanute-Herring biplane. Calling on Chanute alternately for financial help or for a job, he eventually built a biplane powered with a two-cylinder compressed-air engine. On October 11, 1898, he tested it for the first time on a Lake Michigan beachfront near St. Joseph, Michigan, in the presence of several witnesses.

"It was really flying," wrote a correspondent for the Chicago *Record.* "Already the machine had covered a distance of 50 or 60 feet when the speed perceptibly slackened and a little farther on the apparatus came gently to rest on the sand."

Herring had actually covered about 50 feet in six or seven seconds. A

Augustus Herring, having parted ways with Chanute, tests his own version of the biplane glider on the Indiana dunes in September 1897.

week and a half later he tried again, remaining in the air for some eight to 10 seconds while traveling a distance of 73 feet—and convincing himself that he was the first to fly a powered, heavier-than-air machine.

But Herring had not truly flown; his flight had been little more than a powered glide. Taken together, his two trips measured less than Clément Ader's 165-foot hop in 1890. There is no evidence that in either test he landed at a level as high as his starting point, nor did he proceed far enough to demonstrate that his craft was really moving under its own power. Indeed, when getting his lightweight machine off the ground, Herring stood upright and then took several steps into the wind, just as he did with his unpowered gliders. And once he was aloft, he found that steering and control were extremely difficult. Like Maxim and Ader before him, Herring had risen into the air but had failed to achieve powered, sustained flight.

He came tantalizingly close, however, and men like Octave Chanute remained convinced that further experiments with gliders would lead to a stable and controllable aircraft that could be successfully borne aloft and driven in flight by an engine. As the elder statesman of aviation researchers, Chanute would continue to lend his support to any promising venture, and to design flying machines of his own. But when success finally came, it did not come to him.

On May 6, 1896, Alexander Graham Bell stood on the bank of the Potomac River, his camera trained on a launching platform atop a converted houseboat. With him was Samuel Pierpont Langley, the eminent Secretary of the Smithsonian Institution, who was steadfastly pursuing the dream of human flight. At 3:05 p.m. a signal was given, and Langley's steam-driven scale-model flying machine shot from its catapult 16 feet above the water. The craft weighed a mere 26 pounds, and its engine churned out only a single horsepower. But it flew! Bell triggered the shutter release of his camera and snapped the world's first photograph of an engine-powered heavier-than-air machine in flight.

No more prestigious an eyewitness than Bell, the internationally famous inventor of the telephone, could possibly have been on hand to record Langley's impressive success. Bell had been following his friend's experiments in aeronautics since 1892, and never before had he seen so remarkable a sight. The model, he wrote, "rose at first directly into the face of the wind, moving at all times with remarkable steadiness, and subsequently swinging around in large curves of perhaps a hundred yards in diameter, and continually ascending until its steam was exhausted. At a lapse of about a minute and a half, and at a height which I judged to be between eighty and one hundred feet in the air, the wheels ceased turning." Its propellers stilled, the flying machine settled gently on the water, ready to be dried out and prepared for a second trial. It had flown some 3,300 feet.

Later in the afternoon the Langley model repeated the demonstration, circling above the Potomac at 20 to 25 miles per hour until it ran

Mr. Hargrave's box kite: a big lift from Down Under

"If there be one man more than another who deserves to succeed in flying through the air," wrote Octave Chanute in his classic *Progress in Flying Machines,* "that man is Mr. Lawrence Hargrave of Sydney, New South Wales." Largely isolated in Australia from the mainstream of aeronautical research, Hargrave nonetheless made a lasting contribution when he developed the cellular, or box, kite. On November 12, 1894, at Stanwell Park near Sydney, Hargrave was lifted 16 feet into the air by four such kites strung together in a train—the first practical demonstration of the tremendous lift and remarkable stability of the box-kite configuration. A dozen years later European aviation design would be dominated by Hargrave's box-kite formula, which was essentially a biplane.

Hargrave—who never obtained patents for any of his inventions, in the belief that "a patentee is nothing but a legal robber"—built more than 100 kites and gliders. He became obsessed with the notion of inventing a lightweight engine to power his craft and over a period of 30 years he designed, built and tested nearly 40 engines of various types (he is often given credit for discovering the principle of the rotary engine) as well as scores of models powered by everything from clockwork and rubber bands to steam engines and gunpowder. In spite of repeated failures and the lack of funds for building and testing a full-sized powered flying machine, Hargrave never lost faith. "I know that success is dead sure to come," he wrote to Chanute. But for Hargrave, it never did.

Lawrence Hargrave, left, and an aide handle a large box kite during Hargrave's breakthrough experiments near Sydney in 1894.

out of steam. The second flight proved beyond doubt that the first was no lucky accident. Writing afterward to the Institute of France, Bell said: "It seems to me that no one who was present on this interesting occasion could have failed to recognize that the practicability of mechanical flight had been demonstrated."

Langley could not have agreed more. Six months later, when an improved version of his model craft flew for three quarters of a mile at a speed of 30 miles per hour, he felt that his work in aeronautics was done. But the watching world realized that the problems of flight had yet to be solved. Langley's most successful flying machine, while its tandem wings spanned approximately 14 feet, could not carry a man. Langley had never attempted to build a full-sized machine, with or without an engine; nor, in fact, did he intend to. But under the pressure of public acclaim he changed his mind.

When he began his investigations into the principles and practicality of flight, Samuel Langley already was a renowned astrophysicist, one of the most respected scientists in America. Born in Roxbury, Massachusetts, in 1834, he was educated in Boston's public schools. He chose not to attend college, but taught himself what he wanted to know, reading his way through the Boston libraries and serving apprenticeships in engineering and architecture. A boyhood fascination with sky-watching developed into a major preoccupation, and in 1864 he gave up a promising career in architecture to teach himself astronomy.

In 1867, Langley began a 20-year tenure as Professor of Astronomy and Physics at the Western University of Pennsylvania in Pittsburgh. While developing the university's ill-equipped little observatory into a major astronomical center he established himself as a superb administrator and brilliant experimental scientist, and in 1887 he was asked to serve part time as Assistant Secretary of the Smithsonian Institution. Four years later he was named to the prestigious post of Secretary and he moved to Washington.

Langley had always been interested in aeronautics, and he began a scientific investigation of the subject shortly before taking up his duties with the Smithsonian. For the first few years, his work followed the fairly familiar route of whirling-arm studies of aerodynamic phenomena and the construction of small flying models of various configurations. But Langley enjoyed advantages over other experimenters in the funds and resources at his disposal. His shopwork and experiments were undertaken by a full-time staff, first in Pittsburgh and later in Washington. His "whirling table" consisted of two 30-foot arms driven at speeds up to 70 miles per hour by a 10-horsepower steam engine; his small models, driven by rubber bands and with a typical wingspread of about three feet, numbered almost 100 before he decided that there was little to learn from them.

Langley was soon convinced that mechanical flight was theoretically possible with engine types already available, though he gave little

Samuel Langley's model tandem-winged monoplane, Aerodrome No. 5, is launched from a catapult (above) on May 6, 1896. It made the spiraling flight shown on the map at right. Six months later, No. 6, also a model, flew farther and faster, describing the broad arc shown on the map and landing gently on the Potomac River.

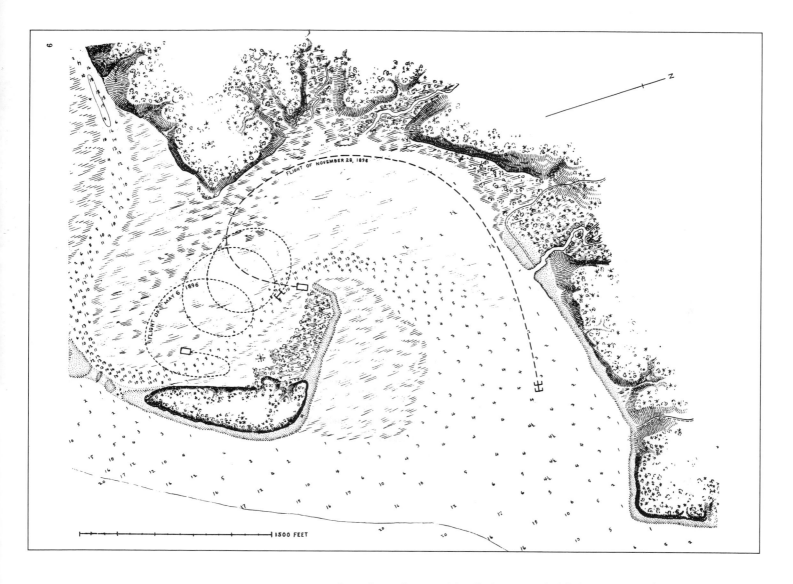

FLIGHT OF NOVEMBER 28, 1896

FLIGHT OF MAY 6, 1896

1500 FEET

thought to the need for flight control. All that was needed, he felt, was to devise a lightweight engine and a vehicle that could be driven into the air. To this end, Langley set out to experiment with larger, steam-powered models; the idea of building gliders to study balance in the air never crossed his mind.

The nation's most influential scientist marshaled his resources, obtaining grants to help finance his work and putting together a team of engineers, machinists and artisans to design and build a practical machine. Casting about for a word to describe his endeavors, he settled on "aerodromics," loosely coined from the Greek *aerodromoi,* or air runner; he would call his flying machines "Aerodromes."

For five years, beginning in 1891, Langley and his assistants labored with the closely linked problems of aircraft power, weight, scale and structural strength. As work proceeded on a series of powered Aerodrome models with wingspans of around 14 feet, the secretary designed a catapult mechanism to launch the craft into the wind. He secured this device to a platform on the roof of a 12-by-30-foot houseboat, then

Its propellers mounted on the frame, Langley's Aerodrome takes shape in a Smithsonian workshop in January 1900. He had agreed to build the full-sized

aft with the approval of President McKinley, who in 1898 saw it as a potential weapon in the war then brewing with Spain.

traveled up and down the Potomac River in search of a suitable site for his test flights. He found it near Quantico, about 30 miles south of Washington; there, in a shallow, secluded backwater between Chopawamsic Island and the Virginia shore, he could conduct his experiments in relative privacy.

Langley was fortunate that the public was not looking on as his trials began. His first five Aerodromes (numbered 0 through 4) were dismal failures. All were underpowered, structurally weak and unmanageable in wind of any strength. Either their engines failed before takeoff, their wings buckled or they nose-dived into the water. Doggedly Langley kept on, redesigning the Aerodromes and improving their engines.

Then on May 6, he and his helpers and his friend Bell journeyed again to the test site and witnessed the successful launching of Aerodrome No. 5, whose unmanned 90-second flight of more than half a mile was so vividly described by Bell. When Aerodrome No. 6 topped its predecessor's record six months later, remaining airborne for 1 minute 45 seconds, Langley's considerable expenditure of money, time and effort had paid off. He had proved the possibility of mechanical flight, which was all that he had set out to do.

Though he had resolved to pursue his investigations no further, Langley now was incurably bitten by the flight bug. The success of his two steam-powered models convinced him that he could build and fly a full-scale man-carrying version. He was prepared to stake his professional reputation on it; all he needed were two or three years and about $50,000 to finance his work.

Additional funding was hard to come by until the outbreak of the Spanish-American War in 1898, when the United States War Department saw the military potential of manned aircraft and appropriated $50,000 to support Langley's project. Langley was almost certain that success was within his grasp. "Everything connected with the work was expedited as much as possible," he wrote later, "with the expectation of being able to have the first trial flight before the close of 1899." Early in that year, the project was delayed when a contractor failed to deliver the promised engines, but Langley was not dismayed. A seasoned researcher, he was accustomed to the sometimes plodding progress of science—and he had behind him the solid resources of the Smithsonian and the War Department. Through the spring and summer of 1899 he continued to experiment with various wing shapes and resumed test launchings of his model planes, gathering more information against the day when his full-scale Aerodrome would become the first manned and powered flying machine.

Langley's well-financed and heavily publicized experiments had hardly given him a monopoly on aeronautical research, however. Other dedicated men, working in comparative obscurity and inspired by Langley's example, were taking up the challenges of aviation, though not all of them shared Langley's self-confidence, or his conviction that the dawn of manned flight was at last close at hand.

Derring-do in flights of fiction

While real-life researchers struggled to get off the ground at the turn of the 20th Century, fictional heroes were riding high aboard a host of gloriously unreal machines in the nickel thrillers of the period. One writer, Brooklyn-born Luis P. Senarens, churned out 1,500 of these futuristic tales. Although he used 27 pseudonyms, it was as "No-name" that Senarens wrote his most popular stories, including the best-selling adventures of Frank Reade Jr. *(pages 104-105)*. Whether threatened by wild men or wild animals, Reade and other intrepid fellows like Jack Wright *(following page)* and the Young Inventors *(below)* invariably escaped in the nick of time by taking to the air.

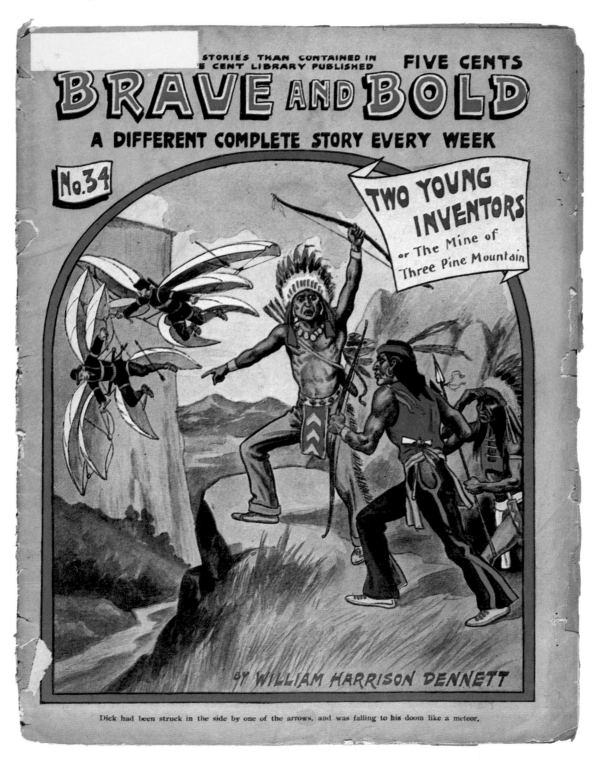

Three pairs of wings apiece get the Young Inventors airborne, but cannot ward off a well-aimed arrow.

Looking more seaworthy than airworthy, Jack Wright's electric schooner saves two adventurers from agitated savages.

PLUCK AND LUCK

COMPLETE STORIES OF ADVENTURE.

Issued Weekly—By Subscription $2.50 per year. Entered as Second Class Matter at the New York Post Office, by Frank Tousey

No. 76.   NEW YORK, NOVEMBER 15, 1899.   Price 5 Cents

THE ROCKET;
OR
ADVENTURES IN THE AIR.
BY ALLYN DRAPER.

The Rocket mounted up in the air, and soared away. "Good-by, cried Harry. Tell the justice I'll report next year for sentence. I live in the moon." The three men were dumfounded.

Frustrated pursuers stand agape as their quarry lifts off for a trip to the moon in a whirligig rocket.

FRANK READE

WEEKLY MAGAZINE,

Containing Stories of Adventures on Land, Sea & in the Air.

Issued Weekly—By Subscription $2.50 per year   Application made for Second-Class Entry at N. Y. Post-Office.

No. 10.   NEW YORK, JANUARY 2, 1903.   Price 5 Cents.

FRANK READE, JR. AND HIS ELECTRIC AIR BOAT
OR, HUNTING WILD BEASTS FOR A CIRCUS.
By "NONAME"

Striking against Shadrach's body, the lion knocked him down, and opening its red mouth, it made an attempt to bite him. But the lion tamer did not flinch. He quickly rammed his arm in its mouth.

A lion tamer is elbow-deep in trouble with a beast he wants to bring back alive in Frank Reade's air boat.

FRANK READE

WEEKLY MAGAZINE,

Containing Stories of Adventures on Land, Sea & in the Air.

Issued Weekly—By Subscription $2.50 per year. Application made for Second-Class Entry at N. Y. Post-Office.

No. 34.   NEW YORK, JUNE 19, 1903.   Price 5 Cents.

AROUND THE HORIZON — FOR — TEN THOUSAND MILES !

OR, FRANK READE. JR'S MOST WONDEFUL TRIP.

BY. "NONAME".

Frank smiled grimly and dropped the bomb. It fell in the foremost rank of the outlaws. The result was thrilling. There was a terrific explosion. Shattered human forms went flying into the air. A hole was blown in the earth.

The fort is saved from attacking outlaws by the timely arrival of Frank Reade's submarine-like bomber.

4

The bishop's inventive sons

On May 30, 1899, the 32-year-old Wilbur Wright wrote to the Smithsonian Institution requesting information about published material on aeronautics. He was firmly convinced that human flight was possible, he explained, and intended to make a systematic study of the problem and then move on to practical experiments. He added that, while he was an aviation enthusiast, he was "not a crank in the sense that I have some pet theories as to the proper construction of a flying machine." And he was modest enough to make no overly optimistic claims about his prospects. "I wish to avail myself of all that is already known," he said, "and then if possible add my mite to help the future worker who will attain final success."

Wilbur's younger brother, Orville, was also an aviation enthusiast. Wilbur would later recall that the two had first become interested in flight in 1878, when their father came home one evening with a small object partly concealed in his hands. "Before we could see what it was," wrote Orville, "he tossed it into the air. Instead of falling to the floor, as we expected, it flew across the room until it struck the ceiling, where it fluttered awhile, and finally sank to the floor."

The enchanting toy, which was made of cork and bamboo, with paper wings and rubber bands for motive power was a miniature helicopter. The boys wound it up repeatedly to watch its skittering flight, and then built and tested a number of copies. They also made large-scale versions, but they found that these models barely flew. Only much later would they discover that a workable model just twice the size of the original would require eight times as much power.

The urge to tinker and experiment with mechanical things would characterize the Wrights throughout their lives. Neither brother attended college—Orville did not even finish high school—but each had a deeply ingrained inquisitive streak that was nurtured in a home where curiosity was encouraged. Indeed, the earliest surviving communication from either brother is a postcard sent by Orville to his father, who was away on business, describing an experiment with a spout-topped can. "The other day I took a machine can and filled it with water," wrote the nine-year-old Orville, "then I put it on the stove. I waited a little while and the water came squirting out of the top about a foot."

Milton Wright, the head of this experimentally inclined household, was a bishop in the United Brethren Church—an evangelical Protestant denomination—and a descendant of pioneer American families

Wilbur Wright (left) and local fisherman Dan Tate launch Orville on the beach near Kitty Hawk, North Carolina, in a successful test of the first fully controllable glider on October 10, 1902. The photograph, taken by the Wrights' older brother, Lorin, was damaged in a flood in 1913.

that had emigrated from England and Holland in the 17th Century. His wife, Susan, was the daughter of a German-born farmer and carriage maker who had sailed for the United States in 1818. She was a student at Hartsville College in Indiana in 1859 when she married Wright, who was an instructor at the college and pastor of a local church.

The Wrights made numerous moves around the Middle West as the young clergyman rose in his church's ranks. They also started a family. Reuchlin, the first child, was born in 1861; his brother Lorin arrived the following year. Wilbur was born in 1867 on a farm near Millville, Indiana. Orville, four years Wilbur's junior, was born at what had by then become the permanent family home, at 7 Hawthorne Street, Dayton, Ohio, as was Katharine, the only Wright daughter, born in 1874.

Milton Wright, named a bishop in 1877, had to travel frequently on church business. During his many absences Susan ran their home with a gentle and resourceful hand. It seemed to her children that she could make or mend anything: She fixed household appliances, devised ingenious toys and useful utensils, designed clothes, even built a sled for Reuchlin and Lorin. The boys were similarly creative. Lorin devised an improvement for a hay-baling machine; Wilbur invented a device for folding paper. Orville, at 12, made woodcuts and prints with makeshift equipment; together he and Wilbur, who were particularly close, built a lathe for shaping various toys and gadgets. Each family member had a lively interest in what the others were doing and how they did it, and all felt at home with books, new ideas and animated conversation.

After completing high school—he did not bother to attend graduation ceremonies—Wilbur took courses in Greek and trigonometry, studying with intense concentration and reading voraciously. He was also a fine gymnast and athlete who excelled in competitive sports. But when he was 18, this part of Wilbur's life ended abruptly in a near-tragic accident. He was smashed in the face with a hockey stick, losing most of his upper teeth and several lower ones. Extensive medical and dental work reconstructed his face—leaving him with a studied smile that would later be described as enigmatic—but his health declined. For years he suffered from real or imagined heart trouble and from a stomach disorder, and he seldom ventured far from home. He passed most of his days nursing his mother, who had become tubercular, and poring over reading material that ranged from the novels of Sir Walter Scott and Washington Irving to technical articles in encyclopedias.

Orville was not far behind his brother as a reader, but he had many other interests, among them a printing business that grew out of his hobby of print making. For a time, he published a newspaper for his eighth-grade classmates; then he did job printing for local storekeepers. When he outgrew his press he built a new one and honed his printing skills during summer vacations by working 60-hour weeks as an apprentice in a Dayton print shop.

When Orville was not quite 17, he decided to build a still-larger printing press and scavenged around for parts and materials. But the

WILBUR WRIGHT
AGED 38 IN 1905

A two-wheeler built by the Wright Cycle Company leans against the iron fence in this 1900 photograph of the Wright family's Dayton, Ohio, home.

ORVILLE WRIGHT
AGED 34 IN 1905

project turned out to be more complicated than he had anticipated. Admitting that he was stumped, Orville turned to Wilbur, who bestirred himself from his reclusive reading and cast an analytical eye at his brother's work. He made some suggestions and pitched in to help; together the Wright brothers devised a singularly ingenious press that performed superbly.

The cooperative effort was not an unusual incident in the boys' lives. "From the time we were little children," Wilbur wrote later, "my brother Orville and myself lived together, played together, worked together, and, in fact, thought together." Their talents dovetailed so neatly that it was impossible to say who contributed what to their joint projects or to determine which one was the scientist and which the skilled mechanic. The brothers' minds worked almost as one.

The new press inspired Orville to launch a weekly neighborhood newspaper. Called *West Side News,* the paper made its debut on March 1, 1889; Wilbur contributed humorous essays and soon took over as editor. Some of the paper's finer literary gems were provided by a black youth named Paul Laurence Dunbar, a school friend of Orville's, who later became a distinguished poet and novelist.

The *News* was highly readable and moderately successful, and after a year the brothers optimistically converted it into a four-page daily called *The Evening Item.* But the *Item* was no match for the big Dayton dailies; after four months the Wrights suspended publication.

His journalism career behind him, Wilbur returned to his books. Orville began his last year of high school but was so bored with his studies that he dropped out to work full time at his job-printing business. Soon enough, however, the young Wright brothers found a field that captured their joint interest and helped them to bring their shared talents to bear on a problem far more challenging than building a printing press or publishing a small-time newspaper.

In 1892 the Wrights bought a pair of newfangled "safety bicycles," chain-driven vehicles with rubber-tired wheels of approximately equal size. First introduced just a few years earlier, these sleek cycles were far more manageable than the ungainly high-wheelers of the day, and their widespread use had made bicycling—or "wheeling"—something of an international craze.

Wilbur and Orville became fascinated with cycling as a business opportunity as well as a sport, and before the year was out they opened their own sales and repair operation, complete with machine-shop facilities. From the start, business was so brisk that Orville soon phased out his printing shop, and by 1896 the Wright Cycle Company was manufacturing its own bicycles, among them the $18 Wright Special.

There is no evidence that it occurred to the Wrights that bicycle technology had anything in common with aeronautics. But the connection had not escaped James Means, the Boston editor who observed in his *Aeronautical Annual* for 1896 that bicycling and flying presented

similar problems—and opportunities. "To learn to wheel one must learn to balance," he wrote. "To learn to fly one must learn to balance. Why not begin now?"

In Germany, Otto Lilienthal had already begun, and the Wrights may well have read the illustrated story about the "flying man" that appeared in an 1894 issue of *McClure's Magazine.* Yet they made no particular connection between Lilienthal's aerial balancing acts and the mastery of bicycling, nor did they relate the problem of flight to their boyhood experiments with rubber-powered helicopter toys. Least of all did the brothers yet realize that they themselves might have the skills and materials necessary to construct a successful flying machine.

When Wilbur and Orville learned of Lilienthal's fatal glider crash in August of 1896, their casual interest in aviation flickered anew. And the more they discussed Lilienthal's research the more their curiosity grew; almost inevitably, they decided to conduct some aviation research on their own. As Wilbur would explain several years later in a letter to his father, human flight seemed to be "almost the only great problem which has not been pursued by a multitude of investigators, and therefore carried to a point where further progress is very difficult."

The bicycle business was almost tailor-made to support such pursuits. Brisk in spring, summer and early fall but slow in winter, it earned the Wrights the money they needed and gave them time to investigate

Orville Wright (back row, center) and his friend, the future poet Paul Laurence Dunbar (back row, far left), are pictured with the Dayton Central High School class of 1891. The two youths collaborated on the West Side News, the second of three newspapers (right) published by Orville while he was still in school.

whatever aroused their lively curiosity. They began their research by combing through local libraries in a search for books and articles on flight, turning up descriptions of the work of Sir George Cayley and Alphonse Pénaud. They also read Étienne Marey's classic *Animal Mechanism* and were enthralled by its photographic sequences of birds in flight. Studying the pictures of wing movements, the brothers marveled at the graceful complexity of natural flight and spent many hours peering through field glasses to observe soaring birds. "We could not understand that there was anything about a bird that would enable it to fly that could not be built on a larger scale and used by man," Wilbur said later. "If the bird's wings could sustain it in the air without the use of any muscular effort, we did not see why man could not be sustained by the same means."

By the spring of 1899, the Wrights had read everything they could find in the Dayton area. Knowing of Samuel Langley's experiments with flying models, Wilbur wrote to the Smithsonian and soon received four pamphlets and a list of other works on flight. The brothers plunged into an intensive and methodical course of study, reading Langley's *Experiments in Aerodynamics* and *Story of Experiments in Mechanical Flight,* James Means's *Aeronautical Annuals* for 1895, 1896 and 1897, and Octave Chanute's *Progress in Flying Machines.*

They also read Otto Lilienthal's *The Problem of Flying* and *Practical Experiments in Soaring* and were inspired by his zestful descriptions of gliding flight; and in *The Empire of the Air,* written by a French flight enthusiast named Louis Pierre Mouillard, they read: "If there be a domineering, tyrant thought, it is the conception that the problem of flight may be solved by man. When once this idea has invaded the brain it possesses it exclusively."

If the Wright brothers were not possessed by the idea of human flight, they were surely engrossed with it. And for all their reading, they were struck by how little was really known about the subject. There was no flying art, Wilbur concluded, "but only a flying problem." Groping their way through a maze of unsubstantiated and frequently contradictory material, the brothers were surprised to find that no one had successfully tackled the very basic question of effective flight control. Pénaud, Maxim and Langley felt that human skill was totally inadequate for maintaining equilibrium while in flight and sought to compensate for this inadequacy by building stability into their machines. Lilienthal and Pilcher had gone to the opposite extreme, balancing their gliders solely by shifting body weight to adjust the center of gravity. Chanute had tried to stabilize his glider with movable wings that would automatically compensate for sudden shifts in the air currents, but the operator still had to adjust his position to keep the craft on an even keel.

Overall, the Lilienthal approach seemed most promising to the Wrights. Although they did not think much of Lilienthal's aerial acrobatics as a means of balancing an aircraft, they liked his idea of putting the pilot in total charge of his machine. And very early in their studies, the brothers decided that they would have to master such a craft in unpowered glides before attempting powered flight.

With balance uppermost in their minds, Wilbur and Orville compared Lilienthal's style of gliding with their careful observations of soaring birds. Wilbur had noticed that buzzards, when partly overturned by a gust of wind, regained their lateral balance by a slight twisting, or torsion, of their wing tips. This seemed far more promising than the Lilienthal-style body movements as a means of balancing a flying machine—especially a powered one—but the big question was how to adapt the buzzard's wing-twisting system to a mechanical aircraft.

Orville's first thought was to design the wings so that a pilot-operated lever would raise the front or leading edge of one wing while simultaneously depressing the other wing. Several weeks of experiments convinced the brothers that this idea could not be translated into a device strong enough or light enough to fly, but they still believed that the concept of twisting, or warping, the wing was sound.

Then one day in the latter part of July 1899, while Wilbur was alone in the bicycle shop, a customer came in to buy a new inner tube. Wilbur chatted with the customer awhile, idly toying with the empty inner tube box before throwing it away; as he talked he realized that he had absently twisted the ends of the narrow cardboard box in opposite directions. When the customer left, Wilbur tore off the ends of the box and saw in his mind's eye a pair of biplane wings, vertically rigid yet twisted into opposing angles at their tips.

At home that evening, Wilbur was bursting with schemes to bend wing tips with pulleys and wires. Orville grasped the concept instantly, and neither brother could see why wings of a Chanute-type biplane could not be warped to alter their configuration as the needs of balance required, much as the cardboard could be twisted by hand. Almost at once they began work on a flyable craft that would test their theory.

Like Sir George Cayley, the Wrights started their practical experiments with a kite. Completed within the next few days, it had a pair of wings, one above the other and each measuring five feet by 13 inches, and a horizontal tail for front and rear stability. By manipulating cords attached to each wing tip, an operator on the ground could twist one set of tips upward while twisting the other set downward.

Orville was away on a camping trip when Wilbur tested the apparatus in a field just outside Dayton. The wing-warping system worked so well in controlling the kite's balance that he hurried to Orville's campsite to discuss plans for building a man-carrying glider that would incorporate the same principle.

For several months the brothers worked and planned, and then on May 13, 1900, Wilbur felt confident enough to write to Octave Chanute, the grand old man of American aviation, and introduce himself as the latest member of the scattered aeronautical community. It was the beginning of a warm friendship between the Wright brothers and the aging author of *Progress in Flying Machines*.

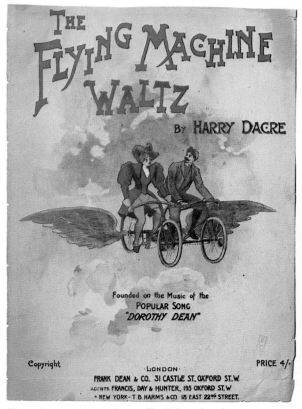

This whimsical cover for an English waltz of the mid-1890s reflects the worldwide infatuation with bicycling—a craze that, in Dayton, Ohio, helped finance the Wright brothers' experiments in aviation.

"For some years I have been afflicted with the belief that flight is possible to man," wrote Wilbur. "My disease has increased in severity and I feel that it will soon cost me an increased amount of money if not my life. I have been trying to arrange my affairs in such a way that I can devote my entire time for a few months to experiment in this field." Wilbur came out strongly on the side of those who believed in practice glides before powered flight and described to Chanute in some detail his and Orville's wing-warping system and their plan to test it in a full-scale, man-carrying glider. He also asked the knowledgeable Chanute for advice and suggestions, adding that he believed that only through the shared ideas of many researchers would the flying machines ever be perfected. "The problem is too great," he wrote, "for one man alone and unaided to solve in secret."

The Wrights were not striving for secrecy when they selected a site for their first glider tests. Wind velocity and terrain features were uppermost in their minds. But their chosen location could scarcely have been more remote. Nearly six months before sending his letter to Chanute, Wilbur had written to the United States Weather Bureau inquiring about wind conditions in various parts of the country. The response indicated that the most suitable place within reach of Dayton might be Kitty Hawk, an isolated village on the narrow barrier beach off the coast of North Carolina just a few miles from Roanoke Island, the site of the ill-fated first English settlement in America. For further information the brothers wrote to the Kitty Hawk weather station, cautiously explaining that they intended to conduct experiments in "scientific kite flying."

Joseph J. Dosher, chief of the little weather station, replied. "The beach here is about one mile wide, clear of trees or high hills and extends for nearly 60 miles same condition," he wrote. "The wind blows mostly from the north and northeast September and October. I am sorry to say you could not rent a house here, so you will have to bring tents." Dosher also referred the Wrights' letter to his neighbor, Postmaster William J. Tate, who was regarded as Kitty Hawk's leading citizen. Tate provided more details, assuring the Wrights that at Kitty Hawk they could experiment on "a stretch of sandy land one mile by five with a bare hill in center 80 feet high, not a tree or bush anywhere to break the evenness of the wind current."

Convinced that they had found the ideal location, the Wrights decided to take their machine to Kitty Hawk as soon as business permitted. Wilbur planned to go on ahead and start assembling the glider. Later, after arrangements were made for taking care of the bicycle shop, Orville would join his brother on the barren sand dunes.

Wilbur reached Kitty Hawk on September 13, 1900. He had made a harrowing 40-mile run from Elizabeth City on the mainland in a leaky fishing schooner, but his baggage was intact—including the test glider's precut ribs, spars and white French sateen wing coverings. Wilbur would have few diversions as he spent the next two weeks assembling the glider and waiting for Orville to arrive from Dayton. There was nothing much at Kitty Hawk except the small weather station, the post office and perhaps a score of lonely houses that were periodically smothered by blowing sand. There was also a tiny outpost of the United States Lifesaving Service, which later became part of the Coast Guard.

Wilbur arranged to lodge with the Tates until Orville showed up with tents and other camping gear. And he went immediately to work. With a horse and cart borrowed from the obliging Bill Tate, he hauled his tools and materials to a level site about a half mile from the Tate house. There he set up shop under a makeshift canvas lean-to and began to assemble the prefabricated glider, meticulously remeasuring and retesting every piece before fitting the parts together.

Orville arrived on September 28, bringing with him a large tent, a couple of cots, and supplies of such staples as coffee, tea and sugar. A week later the brothers had established themselves in a 12-by-22-foot tent hitched to a scraggly tree. Working together, they finished the glider within the next day or two.

In essence, it was a large kite, much like the one they had built in 1899 but about three times the size. They had determined the dimensions of the machine and the configuration of its wings on the basis of Lilienthal's lift tables. The arched wings spanned about 17 feet and had a chord— or straight-line width—of five feet. An 18-inch-wide section in the center of the lower wing had been left bare of fabric, providing a hollow in which the operator was to lie prone to reduce wind resistance. The wings were curved to a depth of two and a half inches, giving a camber of about 1 in 23—that is, the width of the wing was 23 times the distance between the chord and the highest point on the arched underside of the wing. The superposed wings were joined by five-foot struts and braced across the front and rear in the manner of Chanute's bridge-type truss. The tips were left untrussed to allow for warping.

Instead of a tail, the glider had a movable horizontal surface, or elevator, protruding from the front. The Wrights called this device a horizontal rudder; its function was to control the climb or descent of the machine, preventing the kind of sudden, uncontrollable dive that had caused the death of Lilienthal. The pilot would regulate the elevator with a hand lever; the wing-warping mechanism would be activated by pressure on a bar at his feet.

Because of high winds, the brothers were forced at first to test their kitelike glider's controls by sending it up unmanned and managing it from the ground. After one such trial on October 10, the Wrights reeled their machine down to make some adjustments to the control lines and then watched in horror as the wind snatched it up again and slammed it to the ground some 20 feet away. The glider was so badly shattered that the brothers considered packing up and going home, but the next morning they doggedly set to work to put it together again.

A week later they were ready to resume their tests, and they launched their machine once again as a kite. Varying their experiments now, they

A few wind-sculpted trees offer the only relief in the desolate landscape on which the Wrights first pitched their tent at Kitty Hawk in 1900.

The Bible told him so

In the summer of 1901, the Reverend Burrell Cannon, a Texas sawmiller and Baptist minister, formed the Ezekiel Airship Manufacturing Company with 11 other men. Their purpose was to build the flying machine shown on the firm's stock certificate below. Cannon based his invention on an Old Testament description of God's fiery chariot as it appeared to the awe-struck prophet Ezekiel. But the only chariot-like features of Cannon's airship were wheels, and even these were rather strange: Driven by a kerosene engine, they were supposed to propel and steer the craft by wafting fans in the air.

Second-hand accounts of the craft's test flight in 1902 reported that it took off under its own power and went about 160 feet. Most authorities, however, prefer Cannon's own assessment of his creation's performance: "God never willed that this airship should fly."

Stock in the airship company founded by the Reverend Burrell Cannon (above) once attracted bids of 10 times its face value.

flew the glider sometimes empty and sometimes loaded with up to 75 pounds of chains, sometimes with the elevator in front and sometimes at the rear. They were not altogether sure what they were learning, but they were beginning to get a feel for balancing the machine in flight.

Finally, the wind was right for manned gliding. With the help of Bill Tate, the brothers lugged their craft to the dunes of Kill Devil Hills, about four miles south of their camp, and dragged it up a huge pile of shifting sand that loomed even higher than the 80 feet Bill Tate had promised them; the Wrights had dubbed it Big Hill. Their simple launching technique would become familiar to all the scattered inhabitants of Kill Devil Hills and Kitty Hawk: One of the Wrights would lie prone on the lower wing while the other Wright and Bill Tate—or, on occasion, his half-brother, Dan—would grab the wing tips and run the machine downhill into the wind until it skimmed through the air of its own accord.

At first the Wrights had feared that landing face down might be dangerous for the pilot. But a few preliminary glides showed that the elevator allowed such excellent horizontal control that the man on the machine was able to bring the craft to a gradual, easy landing. Even after glides of between 300 and 400 feet and at landing speeds of nearly 30 miles per hour, the brothers found the prone position so safe and comfortable that they decided to make it standard in future tests. They also determined to keep the elevator up front, certain that it provided absolute protection against nose dives.

On October 23, the Wrights broke camp and headed home, though they were still not quite sure what they had accomplished. There had been times, as Orville wrote to his sister, Katharine, when "Will was so mixed up he couldn't even theorize." Perhaps the biggest puzzle of all was the failure of the glider's cambered wings to produce the lift indicated by Lilienthal's detailed tables. It occurred to the Wrights that the Lilienthal data might be wrong, but a more likely explanation seemed to be that the wings were not sufficiently cambered. Otherwise, the brothers were exhilarated by their first season at Kitty Hawk. The front elevator had performed admirably, and the tests had proved the effectiveness of wing warping as a means of maintaining lateral balance.

The Wrights had barely arrived back in Dayton before they began designing an improved glider—its wings more deeply cambered—and planning for a return to Kitty Hawk in 1901. As they studied the most recent aeronautical literature and exchanged a brisk technical correspondence with Octave Chanute, the brothers came to the awesome and startling conclusion that they were closer to the secret of flight than any other investigators.

Believing that success just might be within their reach, the Wright brothers were now spurred to single-minded effort. They made and checked innumerable calculations, thrashed out questions well into the night, shaped and fitted materials in the workshop over the store. They had planned originally to return to Kitty Hawk in September of 1901 for a six-week test period. Now, with mounting excitement, the Wrights

advanced the date to July, and in mid-June they hired a skilled mechanic named Charles Taylor as their first full-time employee. Taylor would mind the bicycle shop in the brothers' absence, and leave them free even while in Dayton to devote more time to their aeronautical work.

The Wright brothers who arrived at Kitty Hawk on July 10, 1901, were far more confident than the two beginners who had test-flown their first kite-glider over the dunes the year before. They were already making names for themselves in the aviation community. A British and a German journal had published technical articles that Wilbur had written on gliding; Octave Chanute had described the work of "Messrs. Wilbur and Orville Wright" in a respected American engineering magazine. Chanute himself had visited the brothers in Dayton at their invitation, and was planning to spend a week or so with them at their camp.

There would be other company, too. One of Chanute's protégés, Edward C. Huffaker of Chuckey City, Tennessee, had built an experimental glider at the older man's expense, and the Wrights had some-

Dan Tate and his family sit for the Wrights' camera on the porch of the Kitty Hawk Post Office, where Dan's half-brother, Bill, was postmaster. Dan did odd jobs for the Wrights and helped them launch their gliders, eventually earning as much as seven dollars a week.

Tom Tate, Dan's son, shows off a drum fish, an economic mainstay for Kitty Hawk fishermen, in front of the Wrights' 1900 glider. Orville wrote home that young Tom could "tell more big yarns than any kid of his size I ever saw."

what reluctantly agreed to accept Huffaker as an assistant and help him test his machine. Yet another assistant provided by Chanute was one George A. Spratt of Coatesville, Pennsylvania, who had studied aerodynamics but had never observed any practical gliding tests.

Camping arrangements would also be different this year. The camp was to be established four miles south of Kitty Hawk at Kill Devil Hills, near the great dune from which the Wrights had launched their craft as a glider the previous year. Since their new machine would be much larger than the 1900 version—a larger and heavier glider, in fact, than anyone had ever attempted to fly—a spacious shed rather than a tent would be used to house both the glider and the camping party. The brothers had ordered the lumber well ahead of time, cut to size and ready for hammering, and as soon as the frame building was completed they started assembling the glider.

It was unusually irksome work, for the brothers were plagued with enervating heat and swarms of mosquitoes. "They chewed us clear through our underwear and socks," wrote Orville to Katharine. "Lumps began swelling up all over my body like hen's eggs. Misery! Misery!" But the glider was ready for flight on July 27.

The machine was fundamentally similar to the previous year's version: wings set one above the other, elevator out front, no rear rudder, and controls to be operated by a pilot lying in a gap on the lower wing. To provide more lift, the surface area had been increased from 165 to 308 square feet. And the curvature of the wings had been deepened—almost doubled—to 1 in 12, the precise camber on which Lilienthal had based his calculations.

A comfortable breeze of 10 to 13 miles per hour was blowing as the experimenters placed the 90-pound glider halfway up the slope of the great dune. With Orville and Spratt as launchers, Huffaker an intent observer, and the Tates on hand to lend muscle when needed, Wilbur took his position on the lower wing. The launchers raised the craft a couple of feet above the slope and ran forward with it; they turned it loose into the wind, then watched as it plopped down onto the sand.

The center of gravity, affected by Wilbur's weight, was evidently too far forward to achieve proper fore-and-aft balance. Orville and Spratt hauled the machine back up the slope and waited while Wilbur inched his way backward on the wing. But the second launching was no better than the first. Gradually, during a number of false starts, Wilbur eased farther and farther back until he was lying about a foot to the rear of his original position.

Puffing with exertion, the launchers dashed down the sand hill and released the machine for the ninth try. At first it skimmed unsteadily two or three feet above the surface of the dune. Then, while the jubilant onlookers cried out with excitement, it sailed on to a graceful glide of more than 300 feet.

More glides were made that day and the next, and Huffaker, who had experimented only with models, was wide-eyed with astonishment. But the more seasoned Wrights were severely disappointed. They thought they had solved the control problem, yet the glider had an alarming tendency to nose-dive or to climb so sharply that it stalled in mid-air and threatened to fall backward. On one glide the machine had climbed steeply to a height of about 30 feet and then had lost all headway. Wilbur had hastily hitched his weight forward and yanked at the elevator control lever. The machine had leveled out and sailed gently to the ground.

Wilbur's skillful airmanship had saved him from the kind of plunge that had taken the life of Otto Lilienthal, and the forward elevator had proved its value beyond any doubt. But it troubled the Wrights that extreme and repeated action with the elevator was required to keep the glider from running into the ground or nosing dangerously upward. In the 1900 machine, better control had been maintained with one fourth as much elevator movement.

The brothers surmised that the problem lay in the wing design, and by the time Chanute reached the campsite on August 4 they had stream-lined the leading wing edges and reduced the camber to 1 in 19. Chanute, sure now that the Wrights were on the right track, was scarcely dismayed when he learned that his protégé Huffaker's glider had been a

The Wright brothers' 1900 glider strains against the ropes that tether it to the ground. The experimenters used a "ducking string," not visible in the photograph, to control the elevator projecting from the lower wing. A tug on the string lowered the elevator, which caused the glider to dive when it was threatening to fly too high.

dismal failure. The aging flight enthusiast looked forward eagerly to watching the Wright machine go through its aerial paces.

When experiments were resumed on August 8, Chanute found that his faith in the Wrights had been well justified. With Wilbur once again at the controls, the craft glided smoothly for distances up to 389 feet in winds as high as 27 miles per hour. Its new wing curvature made it instantly responsive to the slightest movement of the elevator; Wilbur could skim as easily above the uneven ground, following its every undulation, as he could glide in a nearly level line. At the end of each flight, the craft descended at an almost imperceptible angle and then settled softly on the sand.

With fore-and-aft control problems seemingly behind him, Wilbur decided the next day to attempt turns, which the Wrights believed could be executed by banking the machine with the wing-warping controls. The wind was brisk for trying something new, but the brothers decided to go ahead. "The control of the machine seemed so good," Wilbur would recall, "that we then felt no apprehension in sailing boldly forth."

But control was not as good as the Wrights had believed. Sometimes when dipping a wing to turn or balance the craft, Wilbur detected a slight tremor as the lower wing slowed and approached a stall. The

Its elevator pointing skyward, the glider lies in a heap after strong winds dashed it to the sand. Although it appears to be wrecked beyond repair, the Wrights fixed it in less than a week, thanks in part to Postmaster Bill Tate's wife, whose sewing machine Wilbur employed to stitch new fabric for the glider's wings.

An unhappy debut for the gasoline engine

The death of Otto Lilienthal near the close of the 19th Century had driven most European disciples of heavier-than-air flight into the shadows. A notable exception was Wilhelm Kress, an Austrian piano maker-turned-inventor.

Kress had become interested in flight in 1864 while tinkering with paper kites and propellers driven by elastic bands. During the next 34 years, he dabbled intermittently in aviation—traveling to France to conduct aerial experiments with the famed Alphonse Pénaud, devising his own untethered kites and publishing an ingenious design for a powered flying boat. Then, in 1898, supported by a small grant from a Viennese aviation association, Kress set out to build a full-sized, man-carrying, powered flying boat. His finished machine was unveiled the following year. It was more than 50 feet long, with three pairs of wings set in tandem, twin propellers located behind the second pair of wings, and a rear elevator and rudder. It was mounted on slender aluminum pontoons equipped with sledlike run-

ners so that it could take off and land on either water or ice.

Kress put off full-fledged tests of the machine for more than two years because he was unable to find an engine deemed light and powerful enough to lift the huge craft. Finally, in October 1901, he decided to gamble on a 30-horsepower engine built by Daimler, the pioneer gasoline-engine maker. Kress climbed aboard his creation—the first full-sized machine for flying fueled by gasoline—and attempted to take off from a reservoir outside Vienna. The craft taxied smoothly at first but Kress approached the reservoir's wall so quickly that he had to swerve to avoid disaster. A gust of wind hit the machine in mid-turn; it flipped over and capsized. Kress was fished from the water by a mechanic in a rescue boat.

His machine destroyed, his funds exhausted, Kress was forced to abandon his dream of almost 40 years. "I just cannot keep up anymore," he wrote. "We will fly, there is no doubt. Unfortunately, I will not be part of it."

Flanked by associates and helpers, Wilhelm Kress (center, hands on hips) stands beside his huge gas-powered flying boat in 1898.

Visiting Kill Devil Hills in 1901, a bearded Octave Chanute and his protégé, Edward Huffaker, flank Orville Wright. Wilbur faces them, standing under the open door of the brothers' workshed. Nearby are the tent in which the men bunked and a pump that never issued any water; the campers made do with rain collected from the roof.

higher wing, still producing lift, would then whip around and put the glider into a gyration that later aviators would describe as a spin.

The brothers were puzzled and dismayed by this new and dangerous behavior of a control system that they believed had been perfected. On one flight, Wilbur's effort to compensate came too late and the machine slammed to the ground, hurling him into the elevator. No one could explain what had happened, but it was clear that something was seriously wrong with the design of the machine.

Chanute, Huffaker and Spratt departed a few days later, leaving Wilbur and Orville to ponder the mystery alone. Puzzled and depressed, they stayed on at Kitty Hawk until August 20, hoping that further glides would show the control difficulty to be a mere fluke. But the problem persisted and the brothers departed for home, almost persuaded that their careful experiments had led them to a dead end. There seemed to be just one possible answer. The Wrights—like all other serious aeronautical researchers of their day—had taken Lilienthal's calculations as gospel and constructed their machines accordingly. But now they decided that the accepted data were probably wrong.

It was not entirely presumptuous for these two self-taught experimenters from Dayton, Ohio, to question the life work of the renowned Otto Lilienthal. The Wright brothers' diligent study of the available aeronautical literature had by now been matched only by Octave Chanute, and their practical research had gone far beyond that of any of their contemporaries. Even Samuel Langley, secure in the belief that he had mastered the problem of powered flight, was faltering in his optimistic drive to build a man-carrying version of his model aerodromes. By the time the Wrights returned to Dayton after the 1901 gliding season, Langley's $50,000 research grant was almost gone—and his large-scale flying machine had yet to be completed.

So knowledgeable had the Wrights become that Chanute asked Wilbur to report on their progress to a meeting of the Western Society of Engineers in Chicago. Reluctant at first, Wilbur agreed. On September 18 he delivered a generously revealing 10,000-word paper on the Kitty Hawk experiments.

No one had ever before given so informed and reasoned a presentation on the art of practical flying, but the most astonishing of Wilbur's conclusions was his claim that there were errors in Lilienthal's tables of the lifting effect of air pressure on wing surfaces moving at various speeds and angles. Even Wilbur, when he got home after delivering his speech, began to have qualms about assuming that Lilienthal was wrong in his calculations. After all, the Wrights' only reason for doubting the German pioneer was that their gliders had failed to perform as expected. Was it possible that the fault lay not in Lilienthal's figures but in the brothers' work?

The only sure way to resolve such doubts was to conduct laboratory research to determine how much lift to expect from variously shaped airfoils placed at different angles to the wind. Preliminary tests with sheet-metal airfoils mounted on a horizontally rotating bicycle wheel convinced the Wrights that their doubts about Lilienthal were well founded. Seeking more precise data, the brothers constructed a primitive wind tunnel out of an 18-inch-long wooden box equipped with a fan driven by the 1-horsepower gasoline engine that powered the bicycle-shop machinery.

Few aeronautical investigators had used a wind tunnel since Francis Wenham developed the device in 1870, and none had grasped its full potential. Wilbur and Orville used theirs for only one day before realizing its value as a means of simulating the performance of a wing moving through the air. "I am now absolutely certain that Lilienthal's table is very seriously in error," Wilbur wrote to Chanute. He also announced that he and his brother were pushing on with their own work and that they had designed a more sophisticated wind tunnel.

The new tunnel was an open-ended box six feet long by 16 inches square, with a glass window on top; inside was a homemade pressure-testing apparatus for gauging the lifting capacity of model wings. After weeks of experiments, the Wrights could predict the performance of any size or shape of airfoil at any angle of attack. "I believe," Orville wrote years later, "we possessed more data on cambered surfaces, a hundred times over, than all of our predecessors put together."

Aerodynamic research in a Dayton bicycle shop

In 1901 the Wright brothers, after two disappointing summers with their gliders, built the bicycle apparatus below to check the accuracy of some tables, compiled by Germany's Otto Lilienthal, that predicted the effects of air pressure on various wing forms. The Wrights' device was a breakthrough in aeronautics: It compared the effect of wind on one surface directly with the effect of the same wind on a different surface, a test Lilienthal had not made.

By riding the bicycle, the Wrights created a breeze that blew equally against a flat metal plate and a Lilienthal airfoil fixed to the rim of a horizontally mounted bicycle wheel. By adjusting the angle of the airfoil to balance the force of the wind on the flat plate, the brothers proved that the airfoil angles predicted in Lilienthal's tables were wrong. But the bicycle device was too crude an invention with which to construct new, correct tables. So the brothers built a small wind tunnel in their workshop *(overleaf)* and designed a sensitive balance to fit inside it. Working for about eight weeks with this balance, the Wrights evolved air-pressure tables for 48 different miniature wings, and from these results emerged the dimensions for their successful 1902 glider.

A St. Clair bicycle made by the Wrights carries the horizontal third wheel the brothers used for testing airfoils.

The Wrights' wind tunnel stands between an aircraft engine (far right) and a workbench cluttered with wing ribs in their workshop, reconstructed in

937 at the Henry Ford Museum in Dearborn, Michigan. The overhead shaft, turned by an engine the brothers built, ran the shop machinery.

Armed with this knowledge, the brothers set out to design a new glider to try out on the dunes. They arrived back at Kitty Hawk for the 1902 test season on August 28. But not until September 8—after repairing and adding an extension to their wind-ravaged shed—did they begin assembling the glider.

With its warpable wings and forward elevator the craft looked familiar enough, yet it was substantially different from its predecessors. The brothers' wind-tunnel tests had shown the superiority of a longer, narrower wing, so the wingspan had been increased to 32 feet from the 1901 glider's 22 feet; the chord was only five feet instead of seven, giving a span-to-chord, or aspect, ratio of about 6 to 1 rather than 3 to 1. The wing camber had been flattened to 1 in 24, and the Wrights correctly predicted that the curvature would become even more shallow as the experiments progressed and the ribs of the wings gradually lost tension.

The control system was different, too. The forward elevator was still operated by a hand lever, but the wing-warping mechanism—previously activated by the pilot's feet—was now controlled by movement of the pilot's hips in a kind of cradle in the center of the lower wing. And for the first time, the Wrights had given their machine a tail, a pair of rigidly mounted vertical fins designed to help prevent the hair-raising spins that Wilbur had experienced while attempting turns in the previous year's glider.

The Wrights gave their new glider its first tests on September 19, and the machine appeared to be such an immense improvement that Orville wrote in his diary: "We are convinced that the trouble with the 1901 machine is overcome by the vertical tail." But over the next few days of gliding, the brothers found that the craft was capable of the same spinning tricks as its predecessor. At first they chalked up this erratic behavior to their own inexperience with the new controls. Still, the problem persisted; then, on September 23, with Orville lying in the pilot's position, the glider was very nearly destroyed.

"I was sailing along smoothly," Orville wrote in his journal that evening, "when I noticed that one wing was getting a little too high and that the machine was slowly sidling off in the opposite direction." More confident now in his use of the controls, he shifted his hips in the cradle to warp the high wing down. Instead of returning to a level position, the wing shot still higher into the air, even as Orville threw his full weight against the hip cradle.

Thirty feet below, Wilbur and Dan Tate—who again was helping with the launchings—saw the glider buck in the air and drop into a sideways slide. Their cries of alarm were lost in the wind, and the machine nosed up and began falling backward. Completely unresponsive to Orville's desperate working of the controls, the craft was snatched by the wind and slammed wing-down against a dune.

Wilbur and Dan dashed to the crumpled glider, expecting to find Orville badly injured. Instead, he pulled himself from the wreckage without a bruise or a scratch. The glider had not been so fortunate, and the brothers spent the next three days repairing it, puzzling all the while over what had happened. For the most part, the glider had functioned remarkably well. But in about 10 of the 75 glides, the operator had been completely unable to prevent the machine from sidling off and hitting the sand with one wing tip. Unable to conceive that the fault might lie with the design of the glider itself, the Wrights reasoned that the only solution was still more practice at the controls.

On September 29, after several days of rain and unfavorable winds, the Wrights resumed their tests, taking turns flying the glider. Wilbur set a record for the day of 230 feet in a leisurely 13 seconds and within a few days that mark had been stretched to 550 feet. On one very slow glide of 320 feet, Wilbur managed to stay aloft for 25 seconds. But every once in a while, the mysterious sideslipping that had caused Orville's crash recurred: When the operator attempted to return the machine to horizontal flight after banking, the low side would drop even lower and the glider would slide into a spinning fall.

In August 1902 Wilbur Wright cleans up after breakfast in the crowded shed at Kill Devil Hills that had sheltered the 1901 glider (right) during the winter. Before assembling their new glider, the Wrights expanded the work space by enlarging the shed and building cots into the rafters.

Savoring the rewards of three years of labor, Wilbur Wright soars through a controlled right turn at Kill Devil Hills on October 24, 1902.

Now at last Wilbur and Orville began to question their design, and their attention soon focused on the fixed tail. This was the only previously untried element, the only addition to the basic design. First they modified the tail by removing one fin. This did not solve the problem, and they were still wrestling with it when their brother Lorin and George Spratt, who had assisted them during the previous year's tests, arrived for a visit. Two nights later, tossing and turning in his bunk after a late evening of coffee and conversation, Orville came up with a solution. The heart of the problem, he reasoned, was the position of the tail fin. Turned almost broadside to the advancing airstream at the start of a spin, the tail aggravated the control difficulty by causing the lowered wing to lose still more speed at the same time that the raised wing continued to rise and move forward. If the tail were movable, thought Orville, the pilot could then operate it like a rudder, angling the fin to minimize wind resistance and help the glider return to normal flight.

The next morning Orville explained the rudder idea to Wilbur, who accepted it at once. The only drawback, he pointed out, was that a movable rudder would require an additional control, placing a further burden on an operator already occupied with manipulating the front elevator and shifting his hips to work the warping wires. But Wilbur had an answer: If the rudder control wires were linked to the wing-warping mechanism, he said, the rudder would adjust simultaneously as the operator warped the wings.

The brothers quickly converted the tail assembly of their glider into a rudder, and after several days of waiting until the winds were favorable, they began another series of test glides. Two more visitors, Octave Chanute and his young associate Augustus Herring, had arrived at Kitty Hawk by then, intending to try out two gliders of their own. Neither of these machines was even remotely successful, and the two newcomers must have felt a twinge of envy as they watched the first performances of the newly modified Wright glider.

The new rudder had solved the problem of sideslipping, and Wilbur and Orville proceeded to put on a stunning demonstration of flying skills. They continued for two weeks after their guests had departed, making hundreds of additional glides. Taking turns at the controls, soaring easily over the sands of Kill Devil Hills, they competed with each other for distance and time aloft. On his best run, Wilbur covered 622½ feet in 26 seconds; Orville was not far behind with a glide of 615½ feet in just over 21 seconds.

Now there was no question about what the Wrights had accomplished. They had started out to make some small contribution to aeronautical progress. But in just three years of study and experimentation, the two brothers from Dayton had surpassed all other flight researchers and had built the world's first practical, controllable glider. When they broke camp at daylight on October 28 they already knew what their next step would be. In 1903 Wilbur and Orville Wright would return to Kitty Hawk and attempt to fly a powered aircraft. 〜〜

Professor Samuel Langley's Aerodrome, christened the Buzzard by reporters, perches on the launching platform built atop a houseboat that also served as a workshop and storage area for the aircraft. At right below, Langley discusses the forthcoming test a few days before the flight, with pilot Charles Manly, who optimistically had sewed a compass to his trousers.

The launching of Dr. Langley's grand Aerodrome

After years of successful experiments with scale models, Dr. Samuel Langley was ready at last, on September 3, 1903, to see if a full-sized, manned version of his so-called Aerodrome would fly. But at the last minute, Langley's crew discovered that the batteries used to start the Aerodrome's engine had been ruined by the damp climate on the Potomac River, where the test was to take place.

The delay until fresh dry cells could be fetched from Washington, 40 miles upriver, was typical of those that had beset Langley at every turn. Despite the abundant resources available to him as Secretary of the Smithsonian Institution, building an engine and designing a lightweight but rigid train of gears and shafts to drive the propellers had taken four years. Then Langley and his staff had to perfect a new kind of carburetor—the type used in automobiles had proved inadequate. More trouble arose after the craft was moved to the test site near Wide Water, Virginia. Wing-rib joints came unglued. Storms surged up the river. In preliminary tests, as Langley later put it, undetected "disarrangements" in the engine "were responsible for broken propellers, twisted shafts, crushed bearings."

On October 7, everything again appeared to be ready. Charles Manly, the brilliant codesigner of the plane's engine and its designated pilot, supervised final preparations as reporters and other spectators gathered. Now Langley himself was delayed, by business in Washington; he would miss the launch. Considering what happened next, perhaps it was just as well.

Engine at full throttle, the Aerodrome
speeds from its launch track atop a
houseboat, only to plunge instantly
toward the Potomac. The takeoff had begun
perfectly, seconds earlier. But the
launching mechanism snagged the plane as
it reached the end of its 60-foot track,
pitching it downward so steeply that Manly
was not able to pull out of the dive.

After the crash, the crumpled Aerodrome
waits for salvage from the Potomac.
Manly, who managed to keep his wits and
pull himself out of the plane as it bored
into the water, was not injured. Though the
experiment had been a failure, Manly
said, "my confidence in the future success of
the work is unchanged."

5
Countdown at Kill Devil Hills

From the moment Wilbur and Orville Wright arrived back in Dayton on October 31, 1902, they began to plan for their next season at Kitty Hawk. The brothers had embarked upon their aeronautical research with only a slight expectation of personal gain; now they were determined to lay quick claim to whatever fame and fortune might come from mastery of the air. There was ample reason for their mounting sense of urgency. Details of their work were spreading rapidly in the worldwide aeronautical community, and they knew that someone else might well seize upon their ideas and beat them off the ground in a powered flying machine.

Already, the French flight enthusiast Ferdinand Ferber was experimenting with gliders based on the descriptions given in Wilbur's 1901 talk to the Western Society of Engineers; before the year was out, Ferber would test—unsuccessfully—an engine-driven scale model. And Samuel Langley had recently written from Washington, asking the Wrights about their "special curved surfaces," and all but inviting himself to Kitty Hawk to observe their experiments.

Politely rebuffed, Langley persisted; in December he asked Octave Chanute to intercede with the Wrights, explaining that he wanted to learn more about "their means of control." Clearly, the eminent head of the Smithsonian Institution was seeking information to use in constructing his own full-scale Aerodrome. He even offered to pay expenses if one of the brothers would come to Washington. Chanute, calling the proposition "cheeky," passed it on to Wilbur, who replied that neither he nor Orville had time to meet with Langley. "We have a number of matters demanding our attention just now," he explained.

At least one of those matters was crucial and urgent: the development of a lightweight engine. Langley had already solved his own powerplant problem, but even with the resources of the Smithsonian and the War Department behind him, it had been a long and difficult task. As early as 1898, Langley had been convinced that a gasoline engine would be the most efficient power source, but he could find no major manufacturing company that would accept his challenging order for a pair of 12-horsepower engines weighing less than 100 pounds each. He finally gave the order to a small New York firm headed by Stephen M. Balzer, who in 1901 had built New York City's first automobile.

Balzer strove valiantly for almost two years, using up more than his original allocation of funds and ruining himself financially in the process

The Wright brothers' first attempt at powered flight, with Wilbur lying prone at the controls, ends in failure after a brief, uncontrolled hop at Kill Devil Hills, North Carolina, on December 14, 1903. Three days later, however, the determined brothers would be ready to try again.

of building a five-cylinder rotary engine that still did not meet Langley's specifications. In the summer of 1900, Langley's gifted young engineering assistant, Charles M. Manly, took charge of the engine project. He worked on it for another two years before coming up with a single, water-cooled radial engine that produced 52.4 horsepower and weighed about 200 pounds. The ratio of less than four pounds per horsepower was a remarkable achievement for the time.

The Wrights, too, had decided to power their craft with a gasoline engine, which they believed could be obtained readily from one of the many automobile manufacturers that had lately sprung into existence. But letters to a number of these firms proved otherwise. There was no existing engine that met the brothers' specifications, nor could one be built at a reasonable price.

True to form, the resourceful Wright brothers then decided to design and build their own aircraft engine. Their previous experience in building gasoline power plants had been confined to the small one-cylinder engine that operated their shop machinery, but they were confident that they could do the job. The brothers planned to build a craft so aerodynamically sound that it would not require a complex and powerful engine to drive it through the air.

The Wrights were aided in the engine project by the fine craftsmanship of mechanic Charlie Taylor. Inspired simplicity was the keynote of the process. "We didn't make any drawings," Taylor remembered. "One of us would sketch out the part we were talking about on a piece of scratch paper and I'd spike the sketch over my bench." Taylor then would make the part, though his metal-working machinery was limited to the shop's belt-driven drill press and lathe.

With this rudimentary equipment, Taylor finished the four-cylinder engine in just six weeks. Weighing 140 pounds and delivering a little more than 12 horsepower, it was not a particularly sophisticated piece of machinery. Even so, it provided more power for less weight than the Wrights had originally asked of the automobile manufacturers. And the brothers were certain that the little engine was fully capable of powering their flying machine.

While the engine was being built, Wilbur and Orville worked on propeller design. The Wrights had assumed that this would be a relatively simple matter. Propellers had been used on ships for many years, and the brothers intended to base their aerial propellers on formulas developed by marine engineers. But the problem proved to be much more complex than that, and Wilbur's laborious library research turned up nothing of value. It seemed that marine propellers had evolved largely through trial and error, and little was known about how they actually worked. There was, in fact, no formal theory of propeller operation, either for water or air.

The Wrights did not have the time to design their propeller by using what they called the "cut and try" methods of the marine engineers, experimenting with scores of shapes and sizes until they found a suitable

A determined Frenchman's attempt to be first

In the first years of the 20th Century, several Americans were striving to perfect gliders and powered flying machines. In Europe, however, only one man was known to be conducting similar—and historically significant—experiments. By profession Ferdinand Ferber was a French army captain, the commander of an artillery unit stationed at Nice; by avocation he was, as the French aviation journal *L'Aérophile* noted, "for a long time the only French disciple of Lilienthal." Ferber praised the German experimenter in articles he wrote and at first tried to fly his own Lilienthal-type hang glider. Then, late in 1901, he read in a Paris scientific weekly of the work of Octave Chanute. Ferber at once contacted Chanute, who replied that "a Mr. Wright has done still better than I."

By the middle of 1902, Ferber had built a new glider "on the same lines" as the Wrights'. Compared to the Americans' craft, however, his was crudely built, "more reminiscent," wrote one historian, "of clothes on a washing line than of a stiff-winged glider." A more important defect was the glider's lack of an adequate way to control roll. Ferber apparently—and inexplicably—had misunderstood the Wrights' crucial wing-warping system and had branded it "useless."

Nevertheless, Ferber hoped to beat the Wrights to the goal of powered, controlled flight. Toward the end of 1902 he fitted one of his gliders with a six-horsepower engine and some oversized propellers. He suspended the entire device from a cranelike tower and, for the next several months, conducted tests of the machine's airworthiness. The tests were not encouraging, however, and Ferber was back at his drawing board when the Wright brothers set out for Kitty Hawk in the fall of 1903.

Ferdinand Ferber tests his powered Wright-type glider, suspended from a huge whirling arm, near Nice in June 1903.

configuration. Instead they would have to develop their own theories and calculations, and use them in the design of a practical propeller.

They soon discovered that an aerial propeller was essentially an airplane wing that moved in a circular course. They already knew how to calculate the behavior of wings moving in a straight line, so it seemed reasonable enough that they could do the same for a spinning propeller. However, as the brothers later wrote, the problem "became more complex the longer we studied it. With the machine moving forward, the air flying backward, the propellers turning sidewise, and nothing standing still, it seemed impossible to find a starting point from which to trace the various simultaneous reactions. Contemplation of it was confusing."

For several weeks the Wright bicycle shop was in a turmoil of debate that led to some heated exchanges between Wilbur and Orville. "Occasionally they would get into terrific arguments," Charlie Taylor remembered. "I don't think they really got mad, but they sure got awfully hot." They also managed to work out the problem that confronted them. Taylor reported that one morning, "following the worst argument I ever heard, Orv came in and said he guessed he'd been wrong and they ought to do it Will's way. A few minutes later Will came in and said he'd been thinking it over and perhaps Orv was right. First thing I knew they were arguing the thing all over again, only this time they had switched ideas. When they were through, though, they knew where they were and could go ahead with the job."

It took the brothers three months to fill their notebooks with measurements, calculations and tables that enabled them to design propellers capable of providing suitable thrust for their projected flying machine. By April of 1903 they had completed a pair of graceful eight-and-one-half-foot propellers. Each of the delicately contoured blades consisted of three layers of precisely measured spruce, smoothly glued together and shaped with hatchets and drawknives. These propellers, the first to be built entirely from meticulous prior calculation, were to be mounted at the rear of the wings as pushers, so that the craft would not have to move through the turbulence stirred up by the whirling blades. They would spin in opposite directions, so that the machine would not be pulled to one side.

The craft in which the new engine and the new propellers were to be installed was still being built, and there could be no certainty of success until it had been completed and tested. Yet the Wrights fairly bubbled with exhilaration as they worked with growing confidence on their powered machine. In an exuberant letter to his friend George Spratt on June 7, 1903, Orville described the development of the propellers. "We had been unable to find anything of value in any of the works to which we had access," he wrote, "so we worked out a theory of our own on the subject, and soon discovered, as we usually do, that all the propellers built heretofore are *all wrong*." They had then, he explained, built their own propellers, "based on our theory, which are *all right!*" (The emphasis is Orville's.)

Propeller design was not the only area in which the brothers had outsmarted the supposed experts. "We have also made some experiments on the best shapes for the uprights of our machine," wrote Orville, "and again found out that everybody but ourselves are very badly mistaken!!!" With an almost boyish sense of awe he observed: "Isn't it astonishing that all these secrets have been preserved for so many years just so that we could discover them!!"

Indeed, with the completion of their propellers, the Wrights had discovered or refined all of the essentials of human flight, secrets that had eluded even their most diligent predecessors. Their control system worked. Their wing shape maximized lift, which raises an aircraft aloft when air pressure on the underside of the advancing wing is higher than it is on the upper surface, thus forcing the wing upward. Their engine and propellers were designed to generate sufficient thrust, or forward movement, to sustain lift and thus overcome the retarding force of drag—created by air resistance—and the pull of gravity on the weight of the craft itself. The Wrights were all but certain that their powered aircraft would fly; all that remained was a practical test of just how well they had applied their discoveries.

The test would come soon enough, but it would not be quite so effortless as the brothers hoped.

The Wrights' arrival at the dunes of Kitty Hawk on September 25, 1903, was all too reminiscent of previous years. The trip across Albemarle Sound in a small gasoline launch was comfortable enough, but as if to make up for that uncommon luxury the brothers found their campsite in more than its customary between-seasons shambles. Dan Tate explained that the preceding months had brought a steady succession of storms of unprecedented severity, as the evidence at hand attested.

"The rain has descended in such torrents," Orville wrote to his sister, Katharine, "as to make a lake for miles about our camp; the mosquitoes were so thick that they turned day into night, and the lightning so terrible that it turned night into day." One storm had ripped their shed from its foundation posts and dumped it several feet closer to the ocean. There were some bright spots, however. The 1902 glider, stored in the wind-tossed shed, had somehow come through unharmed. A fire had almost totally destroyed the freight depot at Elizabeth City, where the goods they had sent down in advance were stored, but the Wrights' groceries, tools and lumber had all survived.

The Kill Devil Hills camp was habitable by the next day, and while waiting for some parts and materials for their new machine, still on the way from Dayton, the brothers started to construct a second building to house a workshop and the powered craft. At the same time they made the 1902 glider airworthy, and soon were soaring in it over the sands.

Their experiments in the glider exceeded anything they had tried before. Long-distance gliding was no longer their main criterion for success: The object now was to perfect hovering flight, the success of

A kite-flying cowboy in England

Improbable though it seems, England's most colorful aviation experimenter as the 20th Century began was a product of America's Old West. Samuel Franklin Cody, born in Texas in 1861, was a renowned horseman and trick-shot artist and a contemporary—but no kin—of another showman with the same last name, William "Buffalo Bill" Cody.

Sam Cody was also a man of ingenuity and intelligence, for whom kites were objects of special fascination. He first came to Britain in the 1890s as a horse trader and performer in traveling Wild West shows. He soon made England his home and began building box kites in his spare time. Cody would sometimes demonstrate his kites to wide-eyed vacationers on Blackpool's beaches while dressed in cowboy regalia—sombrero, buckskin chaps and silver spurs.

By 1901, Cody had set up shop in a shed at the Alexandra Palace, an exhibition hall in north London. There he designed and constructed an enormous man-carrying kite. The invention was actually a chain of kites: Several small airfoils lifted a tethering cable; then a giant "man-lifter" was run up the wire, with the pilot suspended from the large kite in a wicker basket. Cody and others went up in the basket dozens of times, eventually reaching 800 feet and higher.

For the next few years, Cody worked to perfect the device he proudly called the Cody Aeroplane. "I do not wish to assert that I have produced a flying machine in the full sense of the term," he wrote in 1903, "but I must confess I have ambitions in that direction."

Expatriate American Samuel F. Cody is surrounded by his kites at an aeronautical exhibition in London's Alexandra Palace in 1903. His gigantic man carrier is at rear.

which was measured not by distance but by time aloft. On their first day back in the air, Monday, September 28, Wilbur and Orville logged about 75 glides in variable winds; on one glide that covered only 52 feet, Wilbur hung in the air for an astounding 26⅖ seconds. The next few days brought more records, and after some minor adjustment to the tail and the wing-warping mechanism, the brothers each succeeded in making glides of more than a minute. Between practice sessions they strolled over to visit the Kill Devil Lifesaving Station, wrote cards and letters like casual vacationers and worked on their new building.

On Thursday, October 8, just before the hangar was completed, Dan Tate and two fellow Kitty Hawkers arrived with the rest of the Wrights' materials. At about the same time, dark storm clouds appeared in the west and 30- to 40-mile winds tore through the camp. Working fast, the men put hinges on the new door, barely finishing before the storm broke. Pounding rain and howling wind continued through the night.

Next day, as the wind increased, the brothers unpacked the newly arrived crates and set to work assembling their powered machine, beginning with the upper wing. They had only begun when water came up over part of the hangar floor; as the gale reached 75 miles per hour they put down their aircraft tools and hastily hammered braces inside the ominously creaking building. Then at 4 p.m. a corner of the tar-paper roof tore off. Orville set out with a hammer and nails to repair the damage. Wearing Wilbur's heavy overcoat, he staggered out into the driving rain, and after much stumbling about in the wet sand he managed to prop a ladder against the wind-whipped north wall of the shed. Wilbur watched with amusement as long coattails flapped over his brother's head and the wind kept blowing the hammer around so that Orville smashed his fingers as often as he struck the nails. Eventually Wilbur took pity on him and followed him up the ladder to lend a hand.

It was a good thing that the job was done. Fierce wind and rain continued through the weekend, the storm finally dying of exhaustion on Monday. Dan Tate, slogging to the campsite through drenched sand, reported that five vessels had been driven ashore in the vicinity; one wreck was visible from the top of Big Hill.

The weather did not seriously hinder the brothers' plans, for with the hangar finished they could work on their machine indoors. But the storm did remind them that the approach of winter might well cut short their experiments. And they must have wondered how Langley was faring in his own drive to accomplish manned and powered flight.

There was good reason for their concern. While Charles Manly had been perfecting the Langley engine, Langley and his workmen had pushed ahead with the equally demanding task of building a scaled-up version of the successful Aerodrome models. Rumors of the machine's imminent launching had circulated as early as July, and Wilbur had observed to Chanute that it would be "interesting" to know enough about the Langley aircraft to calculate its chance of success. But Langley had kept the design of his aircraft under wraps, and newspaper descrip-

Holding his engine, Gustave Whitehead stands before the powered, twin-propeller craft he claimed to have flown in 1901.

Flights before the Wrights: a recurring claim

In the predawn darkness of August 14, 1901, on a deserted field near Bridgeport, Connecticut, a German immigrant named Gustave Whitehead reportedly climbed into a powered flying machine he had built himself and took off. He is said to have made several flights that night, one of them covering a mile and a half at altitudes of up to 200 feet. "I was soaring up above my fellow beings in a thing my own brain had evolved," Whitehead wrote. "I could fly like a bird." Five months later, he claimed two more flights—one a seven-mile circuit "at a frightful speed" above Long Island Sound.

Whitehead was an ingenious experimenter and mechanic. Could he possibly have devised and flown a powered airplane more than two years before the Wright brothers? Over the years, advocates of Whitehead have cited a variety of sources to buttress his case. Several newspapers, including the *New York Herald*, reported the alleged 1901 flights; one article even contained a detailed eyewitness account. Years later, several of the witnesses issued signed statements reasserting the truthfulness of their earlier accounts, and in 1964 the Governor of Connecticut proclaimed Whitehead "the father of Connecticut aviation."

Virtually all aviation historians, however, reject the notion that Whitehead flew his own powered aircraft in 1901 or at any other time. They are convinced that the eyewitnesses—mainly youthful helpers and friends—were either biased or otherwise unreliable. No photograph of the Whitehead machine in powered flight has been found; pictures of it on the ground, like the one above, show it to be a flimsy, bat-winged device, judged aerodynamically unsound by most experts. Concluded Professor Charles H. Gibbs-Smith, a distinguished authority on the early history of aviation, "The whole story is pure moonshine."

tions were so farfetched that Wilbur gave up all hope of assessing the Aerodrome's prospects. But he must have recalled, with a sense of irony, Langley's past curiosity about the Wrights' wing curvatures and their system of aerial control.

Wilbur and Orville, isolated at storm-battered Kitty Hawk, did not learn until about a week after the event that Langley had tried a test launch on October 7, and that the attempt had been an embarrassing failure. They were not the kind of men to rejoice over the misfortunes of others, but they were frankly relieved that Langley, with his head start and substantial resources, had not managed to beat them into the air. Believing that they had heard the last of the Aerodromes, Wilbur wrote to Chanute: "I see that Langley has had his fling, and failed. It seems to be our turn to throw now, and I wonder what our luck will be."

George Spratt, hoping to be on hand when the Wrights tried their luck in a powered machine, turned up for his annual visit on October 23. In his wake came a spell of damp, chilly weather, but the brothers warded off the cold with a wood-burning stove fashioned from a large can, and proceeded quickly enough with the assembly of their new machine. They also managed some additional practice with the 1902 glider. Then came some disquieting news from Chanute. Langley was scheduled on November 8 to make a formal request for additional federal funds to support his project. There was every reason to believe that he would get the money; it was equally certain that he would then prepare for another attempt with his Aerodrome.

Spurred anew by fears that their own work might be eclipsed by a Langley success, the Wrights dramatically altered their plans. They had intended to test their 1903 machine as an engineless glider before committing it to powered flight. Now they abandoned this cautious course and the very next day, November 2, Orville noted tersely in his diary that he and Wilbur "began work of placing engine on machine."

The engine was not their only concern. At an estimated weight of 605 pounds—without the pilot—the powered glider was too heavy to be launched by ground crewmen pulling it along by its wing tips. Wheeled landing gear would be totally impractical on the yielding sands; the craft would still have to land on the customary skids. But for takeoffs, they decided it would skim over the ground on a small wheeled dolly running along a 60-foot wooden track pointed into the lift-providing wind.

Spratt believed that it was rash of the Wrights not to fly their craft first as a glider. He nevertheless had proved himself a useful helper and on November 4 he laid out the launching track. Working almost feverishly now, the Wrights had their machine completely assembled and ready for preflight engine tests the next day.

The results could hardly have been worse. The engine sputtered and backfired; the propellers would not spin smoothly. Finally, after several stationary test runs, both propellers jerked loose, damaging their shafts. Orville lamented that any attempt at powered flight would be delayed for at least 10 days; Spratt, convinced by now that the Wrights were not going to succeed, left Kitty Hawk that afternoon. He took the damaged shafts for shipment back to Dayton and repair by Charlie Taylor.

Chanute arrived at the Wrights' camp the next day for a six-day visit, and spent most of his time talking shop and watching the brothers tinker with their engine and adjust the elevator. Chanute did not share Spratt's pessimism; a few weeks later, in fact, he informed Spratt by letter that he believed the Wright machine to be "the most promising attempt at flight that has yet been made." The Wrights were trying their best to live up to this high expectation. While waiting for the repair and return of the damaged propeller shafts, they made additional calculations of the anticipated performance of the propellers, tightened up the trussing on the machine's wings, and tested out the starting rail with the 1902 glider. Taking an occasional break from his aeronautical concerns, Orville brushed up on his studies of French and German; both brothers read, worried and argued. They also chopped firewood.

The wood was sorely needed. Winter was closing in with a vengeance; small ponds near the camp were frozen in the mornings, as was the water in the Wrights' washbasin. There were days when their hands grew so numb from the cold that they could not work. The weather was far from ideal for flight testing, and the brothers could only hope that conditions were no better at Langley's launching area on the Potomac River, some 200 miles to the north.

On Friday November 20, they were cheered by the arrival of the repaired shafts and a fresh supply of badly needed groceries. After dinner the brothers reinstalled and tested the propellers, but now they found that the sprockets that engaged the drive chains from the engine were so loose on the shafts that the propellers would not rotate. "Day closes in deep gloom," Orville wrote in his diary that night.

The gloom lifted somewhat the next day when the brothers found a new application for a tenacious adhesive they normally used for fastening bicycle tires onto wheel rims. "Thanks to Arnstein's hard cement, which will fix anything from a stop watch to a thrashing machine," Orville wrote to Charlie Taylor, "we stuck those sprockets so tight I doubt whether they will ever come loose again." Both the engine and the propellers, he added, performed superbly during stationary tests.

After completing a few adjustments and minor repairs to the machine, the brothers decided to make the first trial flight on the 25th. But just as they were preparing to trundle the craft out of the hangar, a chilly drizzle set in. The temperature, already uncomfortably low, plunged even lower as a biting 25-mile wind blasted down from the north. For two days, the Wrights stayed indoors and huddled around their makeshift stove. From time to time they peered outside at snow flurries that gave the barren beach an ominous look of winter.

On the 28th, a Saturday, their luck seemed to change for the better. The weather grew warmer, the wind dropped and the brothers prepared once again for a test flight. They spent the morning testing the engine, and all went well until the sixth or seventh trial run, when they

Its tail crumpled and breaking off, Samuel Langley's Aerodrome noses upward before tumbling into the Potomac River on December 8, 1903. This second public failure in two months ended Langley's efforts to build a powered airplane.

noticed that something was wrong with one of the recently repaired propeller shafts. Closer examination revealed a crack in the shaft.

This latest structural failure seemed to spell disaster. With winter at hand, the chances for good flying weather were growing slimmer by the day. The brothers had heard no recent news of Langley's progress, but believed that they were still in competition with him. There was no time to lose. Orville left Kitty Hawk on Monday morning, bound for Dayton. He planned to return as quickly as possible, bringing with him new and stronger propeller shafts made of solid spring steel.

Langley indeed was still very much in the race. He was moving rapidly toward a second attempt at launching a piloted Aerodrome. Ignoring a salvo of jeers from the press and armed with fresh funds from the Smithsonian Institution, he had ordered repairs to his damaged machine, and his team of assistants had worked overtime for weeks, reconditioning the craft and modifying the launch mechanism that Langley blamed for his failure in October. He was determined that his next try would be successful.

December 8, 1903, in Washington was not the best possible day for a launch. Winter had arrived, and chunks of ice bobbed in the chill Potomac. But the weather was clear, and a better day was not likely to arrive before spring. Langley could not afford to wait any longer. His latest funds were now gone, and any further delay might mean that he could never test his rebuilt Aerodrome.

To save time, the houseboat-launching platform was not returned to the usual test site at Wide Water, Virginia. Instead, it was towed from the Washington wharves to the nearby confluence of the Potomac and Anacostia Rivers. By late afternoon the Aerodrome was in place, ready to be launched. The wind was gusting up to 20 miles per hour and winter darkness was not far away as Charles Manly, wearing long underwear and a cork-lined canvas jacket, climbed into the pilot's position and revved up the engine for a preflight check.

Observers from the War Department, reporters, a doctor and assorted other onlookers hovered nearby. For Langley, it was an almost unbearably suspenseful moment. He was 69 years old and, at a time when few serious men would concede the possibility of heavier-than-air flight, he had devoted 17 years of his life to the development of a power-driven airplane. The stakes were enormous; his aircraft *had* to fly.

At 4:45 p.m. the catapult hurled the Aerodrome toward the darkening sky. The machine shot upward before it reached the end of the track; then it performed a half loop, its tail twisted and crumpled. The Aerodrome dropped bottomside-up into the river within a few yards of the houseboat. Manly went down feet first, clinging to the sides of the cockpit as the machine pressed him underwater. His life jacket became snagged on a metal fitting, and it took all his strength to rip the jacket and free himself before his lungs filled with frigid water. Then he dived, swam clear of the machine, and surfaced, only to strike his head on a chunk of floating ice. Shortly afterward he was hauled aboard the houseboat, where he sputtered curses of disappointment while the doctor applied blankets and dosed him with whiskey.

Once more the Aerodrome had been a dismal failure. Stung by widespread ridicule in the press, a disheartened Langley maintained that the launching mechanism again had been at fault and that his machine would otherwise have performed as planned. In fact—though neither Langley nor the Wrights knew it at the time—the ponderous craft could never have flown. Unstable, uncontrollable and underpowered for its size despite the magnificent Balzer-Manly engine, the Aerodrome had been doomed from the start.

In some quarters, the Aerodrome's failure merely confirmed the argument that heavier-than-air flight was beyond mortal achievement. "The ridiculous fiasco which attended the attempt at aerial navigation in the Langley flying machine was not unexpected," noted an editorialist in *The New York Times*. "The flying machine which will really fly might be evolved by the combined and continuous efforts of mathematicians and mechanicians in from one to 10 million years."

The Wright brothers were resolved to prove otherwise. Orville returned to Kitty Hawk with the new propeller shafts on Friday, December 11. He had read of the second Langley debacle while riding the train from Dayton, and as he told Wilbur the news the brothers realized that they were now alone in their quest. They were the only experimenters in the world with a solid hope of proving the doubters wrong, of achieving successful flight within the foreseeable future. All they needed was one clear and suitably windy day.

The Wrights wasted no time. Langley was no longer a contender, but they still had to consider the coming onslaught of winter. Besides, they hoped to be home with their family for Christmas. On Saturday, the brothers installed the propeller shafts and took their machine out of its hangar for a flight test. The weather was warm enough, but the wind was too weak for flying. Instead, the Wrights positioned the craft on its wheeled dolly and ran it along the launching track to get a feel for how fast it could be moved by hand. Everything went well until the tail frame snagged on the end of the rail and broke. Out of business for the day, the brothers hauled their machine back to the shed.

Sunday was perfect for flying, warm and with ideal winds. But the Wrights spent most of the day basking in the sun and catching up with their reading. They had promised their clergyman father long ago that they would keep the Sabbath, and not even the prospect of making the world's first powered airplane flight could shake them from their vow.

The start of the new week found them at work with renewed vigor. They spent Monday morning repairing the damaged tail assembly. The weather was beautifully clear, but there was not sufficient wind for a takeoff from level ground; not wanting to miss a chance at flight, the brothers decided to launch the machine from the slope of Big Hill. Early in the afternoon they tacked a signal flag to the hangar—a prearranged message to the crew of the nearby Kill Devil Lifesaving Station that the Wrights were about to make a flight test—and trundled the heavy craft to the base of the great dune by the tedious stop-and-go method of running it along the 60-foot rail and repeatedly relaying the track.

Five men arrived from the lifesaving station in time to help the brothers lay the track 150 feet up the sandy hillside and settle the machine upon it. Two small boys who had been attracted by the spectacle of a strange winged beast on a sand dune looked on in wonder until the engine started up with a robust roar; then, as Orville noted in his diary, they "made a hurried departure over the hill for home."

The brothers flipped a coin to see who would make the first flight. Wilbur won, and climbed into position on the wing. With Orville holding the right wing tip to steady the machine on the track, Wilbur released the restraining wire, and the machine raced down the track so swiftly that Orville quit trying to keep pace with it. All eyes were on the machine as it leaped from the track six or eight feet before the end. Orville set his stopwatch in motion. The machine shot up to about 15 feet.

But its nose was too high. Unaccustomed to operating the swiftly responsive elevator in a powered machine, Wilbur had climbed too

The dream comes true: Orville Wright makes the first manned

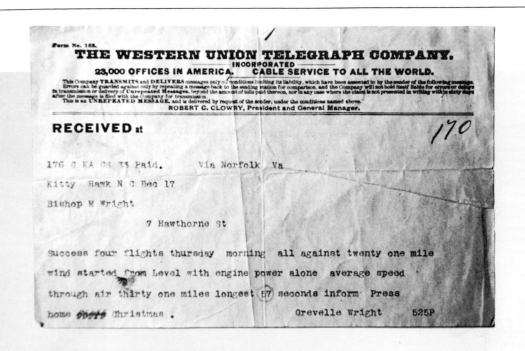

powered and controlled flight as brother Wilbur watches. Later, in a telegram with minor inaccuracies (inset), they sent the news home.

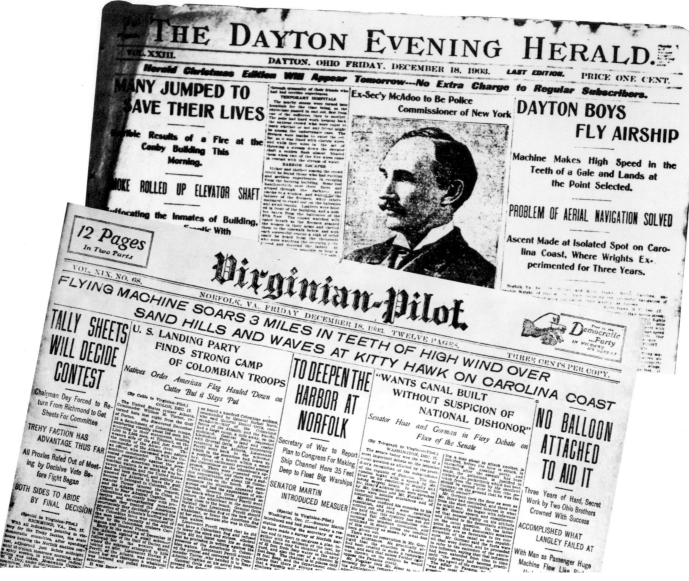

steeply. The stall that followed was inevitable; after three and one half seconds by Orville's watch the craft was plowing into the sand about 105 feet from the end of the takeoff track, its left wing, the front rudder and one of the skids taking the brunt of the fall.

Despite this mishap the brothers were by no means downcast. "It was a nice easy landing for the operator," Wilbur wrote that night. "The power is ample, and but for a trifling error due to lack of experience with this machine and this method of starting, the machine would undoubtedly have flown beautifully. There is now no question of final success." They were on the threshold, and they knew it.

Repairs to the slightly damaged wing, rudder and landing skid were completed on Wednesday morning. Cheered by brisk winds, the Wrights this time set up their launching track on level ground just outside the hangar and moved the machine into position for takeoff. The wind died down before they were ready, however, and after waiting hopefully for several hours they finally gave up and lugged the

Contrary to the legend that their first flights went almost unnoticed, the Wrights' achievement was front-page news the next day in their hometown. An exaggerated story also appeared in the Norfolk Virginian-Pilot, from which it was picked up by newspapers in several other cities.

craft back inside. Tomorrow, they hoped, would bring a better day.

The morning of Thursday, December 17, 1903, did not seem particularly auspicious for a test flight. Pools of rain water lay under thin sheets of ice on the dunes, and a north wind blustered at 20 to 25 miles per hour. But winter was now upon them, and the Wrights had to take the days as they came. They moved their machine out early and tacked up the customary flag as a signal that a test was about to begin.

By 10:30 a.m. the brothers had positioned the launching track—pointing it into the north wind—and five observers had arrived from the lifesaving station. As the engine crackled in the chill air, Wilbur and Orville, dressed as usual in business suits, peaked caps, neckties and starched white collars, stood apart from the other men. After talking earnestly for a few minutes, the brothers gripped hands; as one spectator recalled later, it almost seemed that they "weren't sure they'd ever see each other again." Then Wilbur, who had been at the controls three days before, watched his brother walk briskly to the machine and slip into the pilot's position. The men from the lifesaving station began to clap their hands and shout words of encouragement. It was 10:35.

Orville listened to the chattering engine and whirling propellers and felt the strange vibrations beneath him. He released the restraining wire and the machine moved slowly forward into a 27-mile wind, with Wilbur running easily alongside to steady the right wing tip. The craft reached a speed of seven or eight miles per hour before lifting into the air about 40 feet along the track. Orville raised the elevator and the machine rose suddenly to about 10 feet, dipped, climbed again, then darted for the ground a little more than 100 feet beyond the end of the track. Followed by the tiny band of spectators, Wilbur dashed across the windswept sand to the spot where the machine had skidded to a halt.

Some of the observers must have wondered what the big rush was all about—many times in the past, after all, the Wrights had glided far longer than the 120 feet that had just been covered in 12 seconds by the powered machine. And even now, as Wilbur and Orville stood next to their stilled aircraft and congratulated each other, they characteristically displayed little emotion. But the Wrights knew full well what they had accomplished. The flight had been short, but as Orville wrote later, "it was nevertheless the first in the history of the world in which a machine carrying a man had raised itself by its own power into the air in full flight, had sailed forward without reduction of speed, and had finally landed at a point as high as that from which it started."

One of the witnesses from the lifesaving station expressed himself in more emotional terms. "They have done it!" he shouted later as he reached the Kitty Hawk post office with the news. "They have done it! Damned if they ain't flew!"

The Wright brothers were far from finished for the day. Three more times that morning they took to the air, each time covering a greater distance and gaining a better feel for the controls. On the final flight,

Wilbur covered 852 feet and stayed aloft for 59 seconds before coming hard to the ground and damaging the elevator.

Aided by the excited observers from the lifesaving station, the brothers carried the machine back to the campsite, intending to repair the elevator and then make still more flights in a day or two. Without warning, a savage gust of wind ripped at the craft and lifted it from the sand. Everyone lunged for the machine but it rolled over and over in the wind; when at last it was brought to a halt, it had been smashed beyond hope of immediate repair.

If the Wrights were disappointed by the accident, they did not show it. Later in the afternoon they sent a telegram to their father, informing him of their success. The next day they began to dismantle the damaged aircraft and prepared to return to Dayton, "knowing that the age of the flying machine had come at last."

The world at large learned of the dawn of this momentous age in a number of garbled newspaper accounts—among them an illustrated front-page story in the New York *Herald*—that appeared over the next few days. According to at least one of these confused reports, the plane was equipped with a pair of six-bladed propellers, and had flown three miles. The Wrights corrected some of this misinformation on January 5, 1904, when they issued a terse public statement describing their successful flight tests. But they disclosed nothing about their aircraft, which they now called the "Flyer." It was their own invention, they said, developed at their own expense, and they did not yet intend "to give out any pictures or detailed description of the machine."

Instead, the brothers intended to develop a more practical version of the plane, one that could outdo the fledgling performances at Kitty Hawk. By mid-1904, the Flyer was history, packed in crates in a shed behind the Wrights' Dayton workshop, and Flyer II was sailing serenely over a cow pasture about eight miles east of Dayton. Now that the inventors had a successful powered machine and a degree of skill in handling it, they did not need the unlimited space, high winds and soft sands of Kitty Hawk.

The Wrights had found their new flying field on a large dairy farm owned by Torrence Huffman, president of a Dayton bank. The pasture, known locally as Huffman Prairie, consisted of approximately 100 acres bordered on two sides by groves of tall trees, and was conveniently served by an interurban trolley line. Commuting daily from the family home on Hawthorne Street, the brothers built a wooden hangar at one end of Huffman Prairie and completed the machine there. Flyer II was heavier, structurally stronger, and had a more efficient engine than its predecessor. In addition, the wing camber was shallower and the elevator control had been relocated for easier handling.

Despite its advanced design, the new Flyer's first performances were a disappointment—at least to the dozen newspaper reporters and other guests invited to witness flight trials toward the end of May 1904. On two

The basics of control

The Wright brothers achieved control in powered flight by devising means to regulate an airplane's three basic movements: pitch, yaw and roll. These motions, which are rotations around three axes, are illustrated at right.

Pitching occurs when an airplane's nose moves up or down relative to the lateral axis. A yawing plane slues from side to side about the vertical axis. In a roll, the wings dip to one side or the other around the longitudinal axis. In the 1903 Wright Flyer, pitch was controlled by the elevator, yaw by the rudders, and roll by the ingenious wing-warping system.

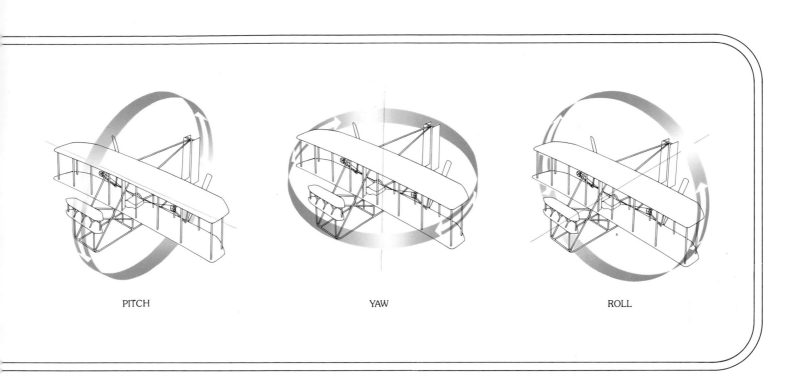

PITCH   YAW   ROLL

successive occasions a hopeful gathering waited for Flyer II to prove itself in action, but wind conditions, light rains and a misbehaving engine conspired to limit the craft to a lackluster flight of only about 30 feet. Understandably, the newspaper accounts of the demonstrations included no hint of the Flyer's potential as a practical flying machine; even the friendliest reporters expressed little confidence in it.

This suited the Wrights just fine. The reporters had been given their chance, and it was not likely that they would haunt Huffman Prairie for a startling story or write provocative features that might arouse excessive curiosity in the community. If the brothers' public failure that spring was a deliberate strategy—and perhaps it was—it could not have been more successful in warding off unwelcome sightseers. Months later, when reporters heard that the Wrights were making flights of several minutes' duration, the inventors still received no visits from the press. "Knowing that longer flights had been made with air-ships," the brothers wrote later about the incurious reporters, "and not knowing any essential difference between air-ships and flying machines, they were but little interested."

Working now under the eyes of only an occasional friend or relative, the Wrights proceeded to test and refine their Flyer. Through the spring and summer they made a number of trial flights of 1,300 and 1,400 feet, gaining valuable practice in handling a mechanized craft, and making improvements in the machine itself.

In early September they completed a device that would launch the Flyer at high speed under any conditions of wind. Charlie Taylor, who helped to build the device, described it as "a wooden track and a tower at the starting end. We drew heavy weights to the top of the tower on

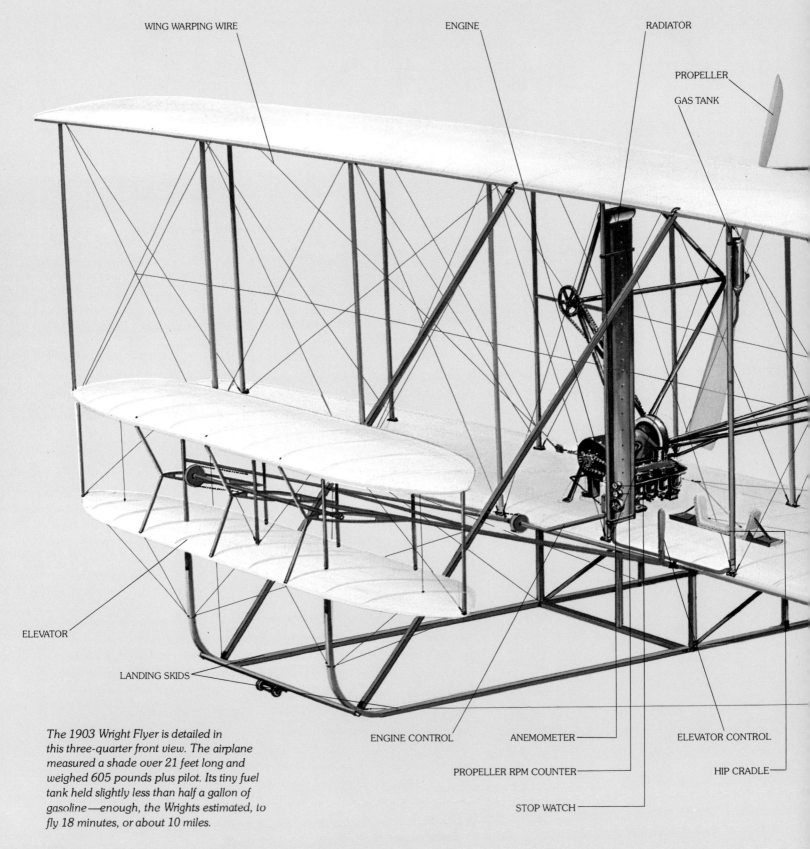

WING WARPING WIRE

ENGINE

RADIATOR

PROPELLER

GAS TANK

ELEVATOR

LANDING SKIDS

*The 1903 Wright Flyer is detailed in
this three-quarter front view. The airplane
measured a shade over 21 feet long and
weighed 605 pounds plus pilot. Its tiny fuel
tank held slightly less than half a gallon of
gasoline—enough, the Wrights estimated, to
fly 18 minutes, or about 10 miles.*

ENGINE CONTROL

ANEMOMETER

ELEVATOR CONTROL

PROPELLER RPM COUNTER

HIP CRADLE

STOP WATCH

The first to fly

The Wright brothers' 1903 Flyer was a marvel of wood, wire and fabric; it combined inspired design and engineering with superior craftsmanship. The Flyer's drooping, slightly cambered wings spanned 40 feet 4 inches. Its spruce ribs were covered with a brand of muslin called "Pride of the West," and its rear-mounted propellers of painted spruce were fixed to solid steel shafts.

The 12-horsepower, 140-pound engine sat to the right of center on the lower wing. To compensate for the weight imbalance this caused, the Wrights made the right wings four inches longer than the left ones, increasing their capacity for lift, and located the pilot's position on the lower wing to the left of center. In flight, the pilot lay prone, his left hand on the elevator control, his hips in the cradle that controlled the flexible wing tips and the rudder.

The Wright Flyer flew just four times—a total of 98 seconds—all on December 17, 1903. Later that day, it was damaged by high winds and relegated to retirement.

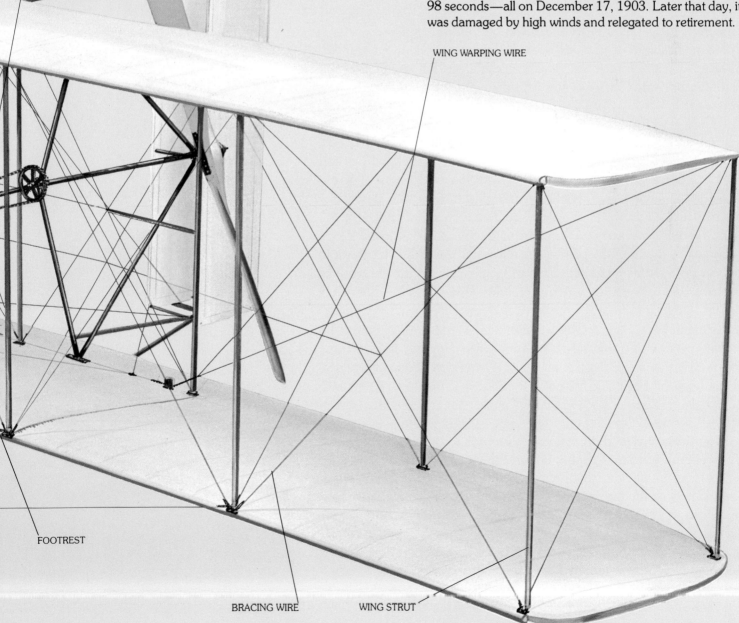

PROPELLER DRIVE CHAIN

RUDDER

PROPELLER

WING WARPING WIRE

FOOTREST

BRACING WIRE

WING STRUT

ropes which were rigged through pulleys to the bottom of the tower, out to the takeoff end of the track, and back to the airplane. When the weights were released, the machine would dart forward.''

After a few days of practice with their launching derrick the brothers' performance improved spectacularly. Skimming at a low level over Huffman Prairie on September 20, Wilbur turned the first complete circle that was ever achieved by a flying machine, covering a record-breaking distance of about three quarters of a mile. Orville clocked him in at 1 minute 35⅖ seconds.

Observing the Wrights on that drizzly, overcast day was one Amos I. Root, who had driven his automobile 155 miles from his home in Medina, Ohio, to see what the Wright brothers were up to. A beekeeper and the publisher of *Gleanings in Bee Culture*, Root watched with wide-eyed fascination as the Flyer completed its circular flight. It was, he told readers of the January 1, 1905, issue of his bee journal, like something out of the Arabian Nights, ''one of the grandest sights, if not the grandest sight, of my life. Imagine a locomotive that has left its track, and is climbing up in the air right toward you—a locomotive without any wheels, we will say, but with white wings instead . . . ! Well, now, imagine this white locomotive, with wings that spread 20 feet each way, coming right toward you with a tremendous flap of its propellers, and you will have something like what I saw.''

Root's picturesque report was the first eyewitness account of an airplane in full flight. It was wondrous enough—coming at a time when others were still struggling in vain to get any sort of powered craft into the air—but it marked only another milestone in the Wrights' steady progress. A few months later the brothers completed an even more effective version of the world's pioneer flying machine, the principles of which would be incorporated in aircraft for generations to come. Flyer III took to the air in June 1905, and went through a painstaking series of adjustments before the Wrights were satisfied with its control system. By September they began to test for endurance. Records were set and toppled almost daily. September 26: 11⅛ miles in 18 minutes 9 seconds. September 29: 12 miles in 19 minutes 55 seconds. October 3: 15¼ miles in 25 minutes 5 seconds. October 4: 20¾ miles in 33 minutes 17 seconds. On October 5, the longest flight of the year—an astounding 24⅕ miles in 38 minutes 3 seconds—concluded only when the fuel tank ran dry.

The first tentative Flyer of two years before had now been transformed into a truly practical airplane. In less than a decade of concentrated study and experimentation, Wilbur and Orville Wright had unlocked the secrets of flight, thereby realizing man's ancient dream. It would take several more years before a skeptical world could fully accept or appreciate the epochal accomplishment of these two self-educated geniuses from Ohio, but there was no way to hold back the age of the flying machine that they had begun on the wind-blown dunes of Kitty Hawk. And the world would never be the same. ∿

The Wright brothers' improved Flyer III cruises above Huffman Prairie on October 4, 1905. The 20-mile flight lasted more than half an hour.

Dayton's belated huzzah

It took a long time—almost six years, in fact, after the first success at Kill Devil Hills—before Dayton, Ohio, fully realized the monumental achievement of its two native sons in launching the age of flight. Then, in 1909, Dayton made up for earlier indifference with a triumphal celebration.

In May the Wrights and their sister Katharine returned from a tour of Europe, bearing contracts from several nations that wanted to build Wright airplanes. Their fame preceded them. Stories of their flying feats before kings and prime ministers filled the newspapers, as had the account of Orville's close brush with death the year before while demonstrating the plane to the United States Army. Motion pictures of Wilbur's latest flights flickered across the screen in a Dayton theater.

The Wrights arrived at the train depot to find their hometown decorated with banners, Chinese lanterns and electric lights. A four-horse carriage took them home to Hawthorne Street, where a crowd of 10,000 cheered their return. A two-day celebration followed in June with three parades, a huge banquet and a public presentation to which all the city's school children were invited. The Wrights received medals from Congress and from the state of Ohio and the city of Dayton *(right)*. A mad dash down Main Street by "practically the entire fire department" preceded a fireworks display in which huge images of Wilbur and Orville were lit against an American flag.

"You must be now pretty well satiated with glory," wrote their old friend and supporter, Octave Chanute. "I know that the reception of such honors becomes oppressive to modest men, but in this case you have brought the trouble upon yourselves by your completing the solution of a world-old problem."

Sister Katharine, in fending off a request that her brothers make a demonstration flight, could not resist a wry retort: "Oh, yes. I suppose a flight would be witnessed by a large crowd, but when the boys were first working on the machine, any number of invitations were refused." The "boys" themselves enjoyed their townsmen's tribute, in their taciturn way, though they said little of historic note beyond a polite thank-you.

Preparing a gala, if belated, homecoming for the Wrights, Dayton plastered itself with posters like the one at far right. Medals were struck for each of the brothers by the city and by the state of Ohio.

WILBUR WRIGHT.

THE NATION, STATE and CITY
❧ WELCOME THE ❧
WORLDS GREATEST AVIATORS

ORVILLE WRIGHT.

❧ DAYTON, OHIO. ❧
JUNE 17 ~ 18 ~ 1909.

The Wright brothers' route through their old neighborhood in Dayton is draped with Chinese lanterns and a homemade banner of welcome.

A parade in the Wright brothers' honor down Main Street features a miniature airship and men in colonial uniforms.

Two thousand school children, formed into an American flag, frame Wilbur (left) and Orville as they accept their townsmen's acclaim.

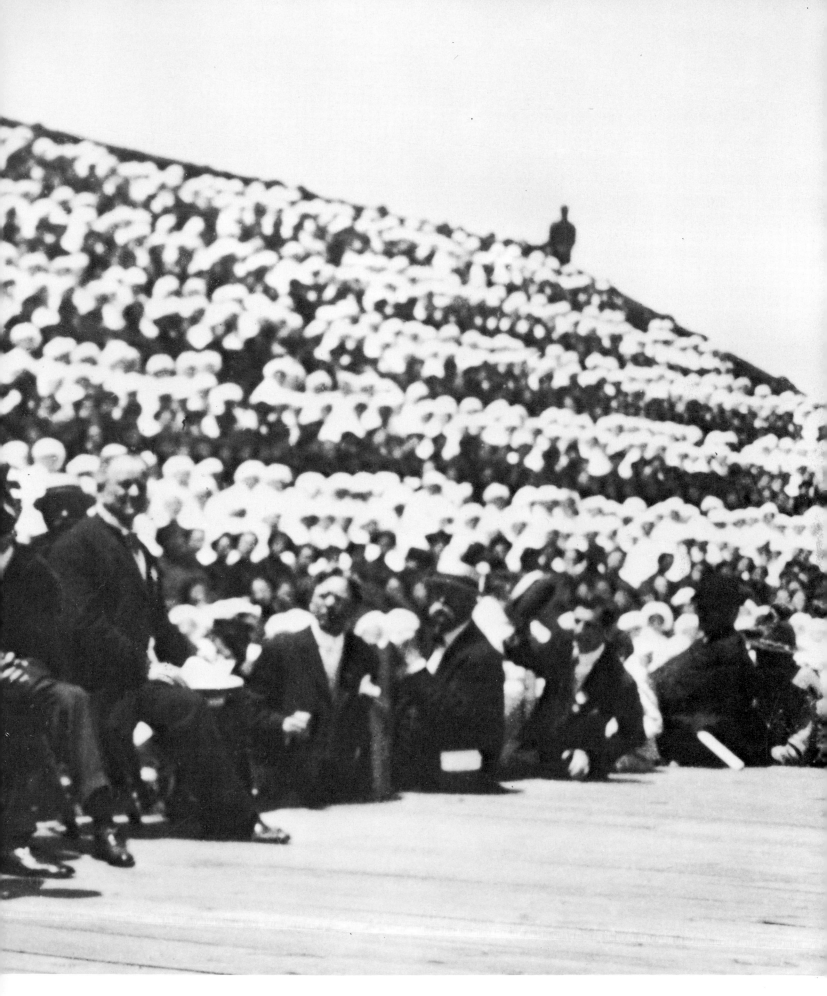

Appendix

Milestones on the road to Kitty Hawk

The legends of human fascination with flight predate history. Man's earliest chronicled trial flights were attempts to emulate the birds. It was only after a body of knowledge about flying evolved over the years that efforts to fly progressed from the flapping of birdlike wings to the development of machines that would carry men through the skies.

Surviving records show that experimenters working in almost every corner of the world contributed to the first true powered flight, which at last was achieved near Kitty Hawk, North Carolina, in 1903. Following is a chronology of principal milestones on the road to that historic success.

B.C.

Fourth C.	Invention of the kite in China.

A.D.

c.875	Spanish physician Abbas ibn-Firnas said to have made a flight with wings attached to his body, and to have been injured because he neglected to fashion a tail.
c.1020	Eilmer of Malmesbury attempts to fly from Malmesbury Abbey.
12th C.	Windmills in use in Europe.
c.1250	Roger Bacon postulates mechanical flight.
c.1325	First known illustration of a model of a helicopter (shown in a Flemish manuscript).
1485-1500	Leonardo da Vinci designs a variety of ornithopters.
1499	Giovanni Battista Danti attempts to fly at Perugia, Italy, with wings attached to his body.
1648	John Wilkins' theories on aviation published in *Mathematical Magic*.
1655	Robert Hooke tests model ornithopters.
1670	Francesco Lana publishes a design for a lighter-than-air flying ship in his volume, *Prodomo*.
1678	Besnier, using flappers, attempts to fly at Sablé, France.
1680	In *De Motu Animalium,* Giovanni Alfonso Borelli demonstrates the inadequacy of human muscle power for ornithopter flight.
1709	In Portugal, Laurenço de Gusmão builds and perhaps achieves tentative flight with a bird-shaped model glider called the *Passarola*.
1764	Melchior Bauer designs a fixed-winged monoplane in Germany.
1783	
June 5	First public demonstration of a hot-air balloon (unmanned) by the Montgolfier brothers, in France.
Nov. 21	First aerial voyage, by François Pilatre de Rozier and the Marquis d'Arlandes, in a hot-air balloon built by the Montgolfiers.
1796	In England, George Cayley flies a model helicopter.
1799	Cayley designs a fixed-winged airplane, incorporating tail-unit control surfaces and an auxiliary propulsion method.
1804	Cayley flies a model glider of modern configuration.
1809	Cayley designs an unmanned, full-sized glider.
1809-1810	Cayley publishes papers on aviation, laying the foundation of modern aerodynamics and containing illustrations of his 1796 helicopter, the prototype for subsequent helicopter development.
1827	George Pocock successfully tests a kite-drawn carriage (Char-volant).
1837	Robert Cocking is killed testing his inverted-cone-shaped parachute.
1843	William Samuel Henson publishes his design for an Aerial Steam Carriage, with fixed wings and airscrew propeller.

1843	Cayley publishes his design of the first biplane, which he calls a "convertiplane."
1847	First test of a powered airplane model by Henson. A steam-powered monoplane with airscrew propeller, it fails to sustain flight.
1848	John Stringfellow produces a steam-powered monoplane that cannot sustain flight.
1849	Cayley's "boy glider" makes tentative flights carrying a 10-year-old boy.
1852	First aeronautical society founded in France.
1853	Uncontrolled flight of Cayley's "coachman glider" carrying an adult human occupant.
1856-1868	Jean-Marie Le Bris tests two full-sized gliders.
1857-1858	Félix Du Temple's model airplane, powered by steam, flies.
1866	Aeronautical Society of Great Britain is founded. At the first meeting of this group Francis Herbert Wenham lectures on aerial locomotion and details the results of his own experiments a decade earlier.
1868	First aeronautical exhibition in history (Crystal Palace, London). First, unsuccessful, test of Stringfellow's triplane model.
1871	Alphonse Pénaud flies a stable, powered model monoplane. Wenham and Browning make the first wind-tunnel experiments.
c.1874	Du Temple's powered, man-carrying machine achieves lift-off from an inclined ramp but does not fly.
1876	Patent is granted to Pénaud for a full-sized airplane design.
1883-1886	In the United States, John Joseph Montgomery tests his first gliders.
1890	Clément Ader's steam-powered *Éole* leaves the ground briefly under power with a pilot but does not fly.
1891-1896	Otto Lilienthal achieves a series of successful piloted glider flights.
1893	Invention of the box kite by Lawrence Hargrave in Australia.
1894	Octave Chanute publishes his landmark history of aviation, *Progress in Flying Machines*. Hiram Maxim tests a full-sized steam-powered machine, which achieves lift-off but does not fly.
1895-1897	*The Aeronautical Annual,* a compendium of useful historical and technical information about flight, is published for three successive years in the United States.
1896	Chanute successfully tests a biplane glider, its wings braced by a type of truss used in bridge-building. Samuel Pierpont Langley achieves success with two steam-powered, tandem-winged scale-model airplanes.
1897	Ader twice tests his Avion III in France, but it fails to rise.
1898	Aero Club de France is founded in Paris.
1899	Wilbur and Orville Wright invent a system of wing warping and fly a kite using it. Percy Pilcher is killed while flying his glider.
1900	Wrights fly Glider No. 1 at Kitty Hawk, North Carolina.
1901	Wrights fly Glider No. 2 at Kill Devil Hills, near Kitty Hawk.
1902	Wrights make almost 1,000 flights on Glider No. 3 and invent a coordinated warp and rudder control.
1903	
Oct. 7	Langley's full-sized piloted Aerodrome, launched from a boat, crashes into the Potomac River on takeoff.
Dec. 8	The rebuilt Aerodrome falls again, and Langley abandons the project.
Dec. 17	Wrights achieve powered, sustained, controlled flight from level ground in Flyer I at Kill Devil Hills.

Acknowledgments

The index for this book was prepared by Gale Linck Partoyan. The editors wish to thank John Batchelor, artist *(pages 46-47, 58-59, 156-157)*, Frank Wootton, artist *(front endpaper and cover detail, regular edition)*, Joan McGurren, artist *(page 30)*, Frederic Bigio, artist *(pages 154-155)*. For their valuable help with the preparation of this volume, the editors wish to thank: **In Belgium:** Brussels—Musées Royaux des Beaux-Arts. **In China:** Peking—Chan Sim-Ming, China Photo Service. **In France:** Brest—Charles-Yves Peslin; Le Mans—Henri Delgove; Noisy-Le-Sec— Jacques Milet; Paris—Gérard Baschet, Éditions de *l'Illustration;* Jeanne Damamme, Musée du Jouet; Bruno Jammes, Library of the Institut de France; Françoise Jestaz, Bibliothèque Nationale; André Bérnard, Odile Benoist, Elisabeth Caquot, Lucette Charpentier, Alain Degardin, Georges Delaleau, Gilbert Deloizy, Général Paul Dompnier, Deputy Director, Yvan Kayser, Général Pierre Lissaragure, Director, Stéphane Nicolaou, Colonel Jean-Baptiste Reveilhac, Curator, Musée de l'Air. **In Great Britain:** Colchester—Clive Hart; Farnborough—Hugh Colver, Robert S. Lawrie, Alec Stenbridge, Royal Aircraft Establishment; London—Nick Morse; Arnold Nayler, Michael Fitzgerald, Royal Aeronautical Society; John Bagley, Martin Andrewartha, Aeronautical Collection, Wendy Sheridan, Pictorial Collection, Science Museum; R. Williams, British Museum. **In Hong Kong:** Magnus Bartlett, Asiapix Agency. **In Italy:** Milan—Sandro Taragni; Rome—Countess Maria Fede Caproni, Museo Aeronautico Caproni di Taliedo. **In Japan:** Tokyo—Akio Fujii; Eiko Fukuda; Susumu Naoi; Miwa Natori. **In Portugal:** Lisboa—Alexandre Marques Pereira, Socieda de Geographia de Lisboa. **In Turkey:** Ankara—Turkish Air Force. **In the United States:** California—Father Gerald McKevitt, S.I., University of Santa Clara Archives; Colorado— Donald Barrett, U.S. Air Force Academy Library; Washington, D.C.—Marvin McFarland, Library of Congress; Philip Edwards, Dominick Pisano, Mimi Scharf, Karl P. Suthard, National Air and Space Museum; Dr. Richard Zusi, National Museum of Natural History; Illinois—Bennett Bronson, Field Museum of Natural History; Ted Young, John Crerar Library; Massachusetts— Chia-Young Hu, Harvard-Yenching Library; Marjorie Kierstead, Harvard Graduate School of Business Administration; Martha Mahard, Harvard Theatre College; Massachusetts Historical Society; Stuart Cary Welch, Fogg Art Museum; Paul Winfisky, Peabody Museum; Michigan—Donald Adams, Greenfield Village; New York—Eugene Husting; New York City— James A. Arey; Anthony Wolff; North Carolina— Bebe Midgett, National Park Service, Cape Hatteras National Seashore; Ohio—Gail Landy, Montgomery County Public Library; Ivonette Wright Miller; Charlene Cross, Patrick B. Nolan, Wright State University. **In the United Soviet Socialist Republic:** Ivan Kostenko, Moscow Aviation Museum. **In West Germany:** Augsburg—Alfred Eckert; Berlin (West)—Heidi Klein, Dr. Roland Klemig, Bildarchiv Preussischer Kulturbesitz; Deisenhofen—Josef Pöllitsch; Munich—Herbert Studtrucker, Deutsches Museum.
The editors also wish to thank Janny Hovinga, Amsterdam; Mehmet Kislali, Ankara; Brigid Grauman, Brussels; Jo Anne Reid, Chicago; Bing Wong, Hong Kong; Enid Farmer, Lexington, Massachusetts; Martha de la Cal, Lisbon; Diane Asselin, Los Angeles; Felix Rosenthal, Moscow; Larry Melkin, New Delhi; Janet Zich, San Francisco; Peter Allen, Sydney; Don Shapiro, Taipei; Traudl Lessing, Vienna.
Particularly useful sources of information and quotations used in this volume were *The Papers of Wilbur and Orville Wright,* Vols. 1 and 2, Marvin W. McFarland, ed., Arno Press, 1972; *Sir George Cayley's Aeronautics* by Charles Harvard Gibbs-Smith, Her Majesty's Stationery Office, London, 1962; *The Aeronautical Annual, 1897,* James Means, ed.; W. B. Clarke & Co., 1897; and "A Thrilling Account by a Brother Aeronaut" by R. W. Wood in *Boston Evening Transcript,* October 31, 1896.

Picture credits

Sources for the illustrations in this book are shown below. Credits from left to right are separated by semicolons, from top to bottom by dashes.
Front endpaper (and cover detail, regular edition): Painting by Frank Wootton.
6, 7: Deutsches Museum, Munich. 8, 9: Ben Benschneider, courtesy Colonel Richard Gimbel Aeronautics History Collection, U.S. Air Force Academy Library. 10-13: Photo Bibliothèque Nationale, Paris. 14, 15: Derek Bayes, courtesy Royal Aeronautical Society, London. 16: Nick Brazil from Aspect Picture Library, courtesy Malmesbury Abbey, Wiltshire. 18: The Metropolitan Museum of Art, gift of Arthur A. Houghton Jr., 1970—The Metropolitan Museum of Art, bequest of Monroe C. Gutman, 1974. 20: Photo Rouault, courtesy Bibliothèque Municipale, Valenciennes. 21: Tessé Museum, Le Mans. 22: Ann Natanson, courtesy Museo Aeronautico Caproni di Taliedo, Rome. 23: E.M.I. Pathé News Library, London. 24: By permission of the Royal Society, London. 25: Photo Bulloz, courtesy Dollfus Collection, Paris. 26: Anderson/Alinari, courtesy Biblioteca Reale, Turin—Biblioteca Ambrosiana, Milan. 27: Photo Bulloz, courtesy Bibliothèque de l'Institut de France, Paris. 28: Photo Bibliothèque Nationale, Paris. 30: Drawings by Joan S. McGurren, based on photographs by David Goodnow. 32: Derek Bayes, courtesy DDR, Staatsarchiv Weimar (Archiv Greiz), Kapitel 41, Nr. 12A. 33: Cambridge University Library. 34-37: Derek Bayes, courtesy Science Museum, London. 38: National Portrait Gallery, London. 40: Crown Copyright, Science Museum, London—from *Sir George Cayley's Aeronautics 1796-1855,* by Charles H. Gibbs-Smith, 1962. 41: Derek Bayes, courtesy the British Library, Science Reference Library. 42, 43: Library of Congress; from *The Aeropleustic Art,* by George Pocock, 1827, by permission of the British Library. 44: Derek Bayes, courtesy Guildhall Library, City of London. 45: Library of Congress. 46, 47: Drawing by John Batchelor. 49: Ben Benschneider, courtesy Colonel Richard Gimbel Aeronautics History Collection, U.S. Air Force Academy Library. 50: National Air and Space Museum, Smithsonian Institution. 51: Science Museum, London. 52, 53: Crown Copyright, Science Museum, London. 54: Derek Bayes, courtesy Royal Aeronautical Society, London. 56: Musée de l'Air, Paris; photo Pépin Fils, courtesy Amis de J. M. Le Bris, Brest. 57: Royal Aeronautical Society, London. 58, 59: Drawing by John Batchelor. 60: Derek Bayes, courtesy Guildhall Library, City of London. 63: Bill Ray, courtesy National Air and Space Museum, Smithsonian Institution. 64: The Bettmann Archive—Hatfield History of Aeronautics, Northrop University. 65: Mary Evans Picture Library, London—The Bettmann Archive; Hatfield History of Aeronautics, Northrop University. 66: Maria Vincenza Aloisi, courtesy Musée de l'Air, Paris. 67: Photo Bibliothèque Nationale, Paris. 68, 69: National Air and Space Museum, Smithsonian Institution; Science Museum, London. 70, 71: Science Museum, London. 72: National Air and Space Museum, Smithsonian Institution. 74, 75: Deutsches Museum, Munich. 76: Bildarchiv Preussischer Kulturbesitz, Berlin (West). 77: Ullstein Bilderdienst, Berlin (West)— Deutsches Museum, Munich. 79: Photo Bibliothèque Nationale, Paris. 80: Deutsches Museum, Munich. 82: National Air and Space Museum, Smithsonian Institution; courtesy Picture Collection, Cooper-Hewitt Museum Library, Smithsonian Institution, New York. 85: National Air and Space Museum, Smithsonian Institution. 87: Musée de l'Air, Paris—American Heritage Center, University of Wyoming. 88, 89: National Air and Space Museum, Smithsonian Institution; Ameri-

can Heritage Center, University of Wyoming. 90-93: National Air and Space Museum, Smithsonian Institution. 95: Museum of Applied Arts and Sciences, Sydney. 96: National Air and Space Museum, Smithsonian Institution. 97-99: Library of Congress. 100-105: Ben Benschneider, courtesy Colonel Richard Gimbel Aeronautics History Collection, U.S. Air Force Academy Library. 106-109: Library of Congress. 110: Wright Brothers Collection, Archives and Special Collections, Wright State University Library. 111: Dayton and Montgomery County Public Library—Library of Congress (2). 112: Henry Beville, courtesy Bella Landauer Sheet Music Collection, National Air and Space Museum, Smithsonian Institution. 114,

115: Library of Congress. 116: Lacy L. Davis. 118-121: Library of Congress. 122: Deutsches Museum, Munich. 123: Wright Brothers Collection, Archives and Special Collections, Wright State University Library. 125-127: Henry Groskinsky, courtesy Greenfield Village. 129: Wright Brothers Collection, Archives and Special Collections, Wright State University Library. 130, 131: Library of Congress. 132-135: National Air and Space Museum, Smithsonian Institution. 136: Library of Congress. 139: Musée de l'Air, Paris. 142, 143: Royal Aircraft Establishment, Farnborough. 145: National Air and Space Museum, Smithsonian Institution. 148: Reprinted with permission of *The Washington Star*. 150, 151: Li-

brary of Congress. 152: U.S. Air Force Museum—Library of Congress. 155: Drawings by Frederic F. Bigio from B-C Graphics. 156, 157: Drawing by John Batchelor. 158, 159: Library of Congress. 160: Henry Groskinsky, courtesy Wright Brothers Collection, Archives and Special Collections, Wright State University Library. 161: Dayton and Montgomery County Public Library. 162, 163: Wright Brothers Collection, Archives and Special Collections, Wright State University Library. 164, 165: Henry Beville, courtesy National Air and Space Museum, Smithsonian Institution. 166, 167: Wright Brothers Collection, Archives and Special Collections, Wright State University Library.

Bibliography

Books

American Heritage, *History of Flight.* Simon & Schuster, 1964.

Bach, Richard, *A Gift of Wings.* Delacorte Press, 1974.

Bacon, Frier, *Discovery of the Miracles of Art, Nature, and Magick.* London: Starre, 1659.

Broomfield, G. A., *Pioneer of the Air: The Life and Times of Colonel S. F. Cody.* Aldershot, England: Gale & Polden, 1953.

Cayley, George, *Aeronautical and Miscellaneous Notebook.* Cambridge: W. Heffer & Sons, Ltd., 1933.

Chanute, Octave:
Diary of Flying Trials. 1896.
Progress in Flying Machines. Lorenz & Herweg, 1976.

Combs, Harry, *Kill Devil Hill: The Epic of the Wright Brothers, 1900-1909.* Houghton Mifflin, 1979.

Crouch, Thomas, *To Ride the Fractious Horse.* University Microfilms International, 1976.

Davy, M. J. B., *Interpretive History of Flight.* London: His Majesty's Stationery Office, 1937.

Edgington, Donald R., ed., *The Threshold of Flight.* Northrop Institute of Technology, 1968.

Fairlie, Gerard, and Elizabeth Cayley, *The Life of a Genius.* London: Hodder and Stoughton, 1965.

George, M. Dorothy:
Hogarth To Cruikshank: Social Change in Graphic Satire. London: The Penguin Press, 1967.
Political & Personal Satires, A Catalogue, Vol. 10. London: British Museum, 1952.
Political & Personal Satires, A Catalogue, Vol. 11. London: British Museum, 1954.

Gibbs-Smith, Charles H.:
The Aeroplane: An Historical Survey of Its Origins and Development. London: Her Majesty's Stationery Office, 1960.
Aviation: An Historical Survey from its Origins to the End of World War II. London: Her Majesty's Stationery Office, 1970.
Clément Ader: His Flight-Claims and his Place in History. London: Her Majesty's Stationery Office, 1968.
The Invention of the Aeroplane (1799-1909). Taplinger Publishing Co., Inc., 1965.
The Inventions of Leonardo da Vinci. Charles Scribner's Sons, 1978.
Leonardo da Vinci's Aeronautics. London: Her Majesty's Stationery Office, 1967.
The Rebirth of European Aviation 1902-1908: A Study of the Wright Brothers' Influence. London: Her Majesty's Stationery Office, 1974.
Sir George Cayley's Aeronautics 1796-1855. London: Her Majesty's Stationery Office, 1962.
The Wright Brothers: A Brief Account of Their Work 1899-1911. London: Her Majesty's Stationery Office, 1963.

Hallion, Richard P., ed., *The Wright Brothers: Heirs of Prometheus.* National Air and Space Museum, 1978.

Harris, Sherwood, *The First to Fly: Aviation's Pioneer Days.* Simon and Schuster, 1970.

Hart, Clive:
The Dream of Flight: Aeronauts from Classical Times to the Renaissance. Winchester Press, 1972.
Kites, An Historical Survey. Frederick A. Praeger, 1967.

Hobbs, Leonard S., *The Wright Brothers' Engines and Their Design.* Smithsonian Institution

Press, 1971.

Hooke, Robert, *Micrographia or Some Physiological Descriptions of Minute Bodies Made by Magnifying Glasses with Observations and Inquires Thereupon.* Dover Publications, Inc., 1961.

Kelly, Fred C., *The Wright Brothers.* Ballantine Books, 1943.

Kelly, Fred C., ed., *Miracle at Kitty Hawk: The Letters of Wilbur and Orville Wright.* Farrar, Straus and Young, 1951.

Langley, Samuel Pierpont:
Langley Memoir on Mechanical Flight. The Smithsonian Institution, 1911.
Langley's Aerodrome. Government Printing Office, no date.

Laufer, Berthold, "The Prehistory of Aviation," *Field Museum of Natural History,* Vol. 18, No. 1. Field Museum of Natural History, 1928.

Levy, Reuben, *The Epic of the Kings.* The University of Chicago Press, 1967.

Lilienthal, Otto, *Birdflight as the Basis of Aviation.* London: Longmans, Green and Co., 1911.

McFarland, Marvin W., ed., *The Papers of Wilbur and Orville Wright:*
Volume One: 1899-1905. Arno Press, 1972.
Volume Two: 1906-1948. Arno Press, 1972.

McMahon, John R., *The Wright Brothers: Fathers of Flight.* Little, Brown, 1930.

Maxim, Hiram Percy, *A Genius in the Family.* Dover Publications, Inc., 1962.

Maxim, Hiram S.:
Artificial and Natural Flight. London: Whittaker & Co., 1909.
My Life. London: Methuen & Co. Ltd., 1915.

Means, James H., *James Means and the Problem*

of Manflight During the Period 1882-1920. Smithsonian Institution, 1964.

Murchie, Guy, Song of the Sky. The Riverside Press, 1954.

Needham, Joseph, Science and Civilisation in China. Cambridge: Cambridge University Press, 1965.

Pritchard, J. Laurence:
Sir George Cayley, Bart.: The Father of British Aeronautics. Sussex: The Lewes Press, 1955.
Sir George Cayley: The Inventor of the Aeroplane. Horizon Press, 1962.

Randolph, Stella, Lost Flights of Gustave Whitehead. Places, Inc., 1937.

Renstrom, Arthur G., Wilbur & Orville Wright. Library of Congress, 1975.

Robinson, Henry W., ed., The Diary of Robert Hooke. London: Taylor & Francis, 1935.

Shaw, W. Hudson, and Olaf Ruhen, Lawrence Hargrave: Explorer, Inventor & Aviation Experimenter. Stanmore, New South Wales: Cassell Australia Limited, 1977.

Spearman, Arthur Dunning, John Joseph Montgomery: Father of Basic Flying. University of Santa Clara, 1967.

Stever, H. Guyford, and James J. Haggerty, Flight. Time-Life Books, 1973.

Supf, Peter, Das Buch der Deutschen Fluggeschichte. Berlin: Verlagsanstalt Hermann Klemm AG, 1935.

Taylor, John W. R., and Kenneth Munson, History of Aviation. Crown Publishers, 1972.

Thorndike, Lynn, A History of Magic and Experimental Science During the First Thirteen Centuries of Our Era. Columbia University Press, 1923.

Vaeth, J. Gordon, Langley: Man of Science and Flight. The Ronald Press Company, 1966.

Voisin, Gabriel, Men, Women and 10,000 Kites. London: Putnam, 1961.

Walsh, John Evangelist, One Day at Kitty Hawk: The Untold Story of the Wright Brothers and the Airplane. Thomas Y. Crowell Company, 1975.

Westfall, Richard S., The Posthumous Works of Robert Hooke. Johnson Reprint Corporation, 1969.

Wilkins, John, The Mathematical and Philosophical Works. London: Frank Cass & Co. Ltd., 1970.

Wragg, David W., Flight Before Flying. Frederick Fell Publishers, Inc., 1974.

Periodicals

Chanute, Octave, "In Memoriam," The Journal, May 1911.

Crouch, Tom, "December: Diamond Anniversary of Man's Propulsion Skyward," Smithsonian Magazine, December 1978.

Culick, F. E. C., "The Origins of the First Powered, Man-Carrying Airplane," Scientific American, July 1979.

Langley, Samuel Pierpont:
"Mechanical Flight," Cosmopolitan, May 1892.
"The Flying-Machine," McClure's Magazine, June 1897.

Lilienthal, Otto, "The Problem of Flying," Annual Report of the Board of Regents of the Smithsonian Institution, July 1893, Government Printing Office.

McSurely, Alexander, "The Wrights and the Propeller," Aviation Week, 1953.

Martin, James V., "When Will Merit Count in Aviation?" The Liberation, October 1924.

Maxim, Hiram S., "The Aeroplane," Cosmopolitan, June 1892.

Means, James, ed.:
The Aeronautical Annual, 1895.
The Aeronautical Annual, 1896.
The Aeronautical Annual, 1897.

National Air and Space Museum, Smithsonian Institution biographical files:

Ballantyne, A. M., and J. Laurence Pritchard, "The Lives and Work of William Samuel Henson and John Stringfellow," the First Henson-Stringfellow Memorial Lecture, February 16, 1956.

Dam, H. J. W., "The Maxim Air-Ship: An Interview with the Inventor," 1893.

"Odyssey of the Albatross," Time, June 25, 1979.

Pritchard, J. Laurence:
"The Wright Brothers and the Royal Aeronautical Society: A Survey and Tribute," Journal of the Royal Aeronautical Society, December 1953.
"The Dawn of Aerodynamics," Journal of the Royal Aeronautical Society, March 1957.

Rae, John B., "Science and Engineering in the History of Aviation," Technology and Culture, Fall 1961.

Taylor, Charles E., "My Story of the Wright Brothers," Collier's Weekly, December 26, 1948.

Vernon, "The Flying Man: Otto Lilienthal's Flying Machine," McClure's Magazine, September 1894.

West, Rupert E., "When the Wrights Gave Wings to the World," U.S. Air Service, December 1927.

White, Lynn, Jr.:
"Eilmer of Malmesbury, An Eleventh Century Aviator," Technology and Culture, Spring 1961.
"The Invention of the Parachute," Technology and Culture, July 1968.
"Medieval Uses of Air," Scientific American, August 1970.

Wood, R. W., "A Thrilling Account by a Brother Aeronaut," Boston Evening Transcript, October 31, 1896.

Wright, Orville and Wilbur, "The Wright Brothers' Aeroplane," The Century Magazine, September 1908.

Wright, Orville, "How We Invented the Airplane," Harper's Magazine, June 1953.

Index

Printed in U.S.A.